A FUNCTIONAL VIEW
OF LANGUAGE

Oxford University Press, Amen House, London E.C.4

GLASGOW   NEW YORK   TORONTO   MELBOURNE   WELLINGTON
BOMBAY   CALCUTTA   MADRAS   KARACHI   LAHORE   DACCA
CAPE TOWN   SALISBURY   NAIROBI   IBADAN   ACCRA
KUALA LUMPUR   HONG KONG

A FUNCTIONAL VIEW
OF LANGUAGE

BY

ANDRÉ MARTINET

PROFESSOR OF GENERAL LINGUISTICS
AT THE SORBONNE

BEING

THE WAYNFLETE LECTURES

DELIVERED IN THE COLLEGE OF

ST. MARY MAGDALEN, OXFORD

1961

OXFORD
AT THE CLARENDON PRESS
1962

TO

AUSTIN GILL

PREFACE

A TITLE is rarely quite as explicit as its author intends it to be, and a preface is no unnatural place for some glossing.

The 'functional' label, which appeared in the title of my 1949 booklet *Phonology as Functional Phonetics* and which I am using here again, is probably no less forbidding to large sections of the philological public than the more usual 'structural' tag. I am quite aware of this, and if I persevere it is because I am less inclined to flatter the preconceptions of some of my readers than to stress what, in my opinion, is conducive to sounder descriptive methods and a better understanding of language.

When reading, with full appreciation, the books and essays of some contemporary descriptivists, I cannot help wondering at times whether, in their striving for scientific detachment and their laudable efforts to do away with vague idealistic phraseology, they are not missing what Sapir, hampered by the pervading psychologism of his age, gropingly referred to as 'a basic plan, a certain cut to each language'. Fighting 'mentalism' should not consist in denying the existence of well-established facts, but in showing what palpable realities stand behind loose prescientific phrasing: it is fair play, for contemporary structuralists, to ridicule a phrase like 'the spirit of a language' because it is more likely to evoke some winged supernatural being than a set of internal relations; but it is bad policy to ignore or neglect the fact that any utterance or any segment of an utterance becomes a linguistic object only inasmuch as it has been identified as belonging to a given language. Physically, a glottal stop is just a noise, but in a segment identified as Arabic it will be perceived as a fully distinctive unit; if the context is known to be German it will be conceived as a delimiting trick; in a French utterance, it will be cough and nothing else. What differentiates a language from another language is not, as still widely believed, another way of combining ready-made sounds (or letters!) for evoking the same things or concepts, with specific but marginal deviations called 'accent' and 'idioms', it is a *sui generis* organization where particular sound types are given a certain role in shaping specific signs. Each of these corresponds to one of the elements into which experience has to be analysed before it can be communicated by means of language and is to be classified according to the particular functions it assumes in linguistic communication. Describing a language consists in pointing out what makes it different from all others. Now, since speech organs, perceptive and thinking abilities would seem to be much the same throughout mankind, what makes it different is less the substantial nature of the units it operates with than the way these units function or, in other words, contribute to communication.

For offering me the opportunity of presenting these views of mine, first to an audience of distinguished scholars and advanced students at Oxford, and ultimately to a wider English-speaking public, my thanks are due to the President and Scholars of the College of St. Mary Magdalen who invited me to deliver a series of six Waynflete lectures in the winter of 1961 and to the Clarendon Press for their willingness to print an expanded version of these lectures.

I should also like to address my thanks to my old friends Eugene and Sylvia Dorfman for reading and improving the text of the lectures, and to Mr. John Ross for his careful reading of both the manuscript and the proof.

To Austin Gill at whose instigation the invitation was launched, who made my stay at Oxford a congenial experience, and who read my manuscript before it went to press, this book is dedicated.

A. M.

CONTENTS

I

REALISM VERSUS FORMALISM

THE most remarkable achievement of contemporary linguistics is probably the final assertion of its legitimacy as a completely autonomous discipline with its own object, aims, and methods. Whereas 'philology' had never severed the ties that linked it to old texts and classical education, 'linguistics', as a practically new term in English, labels its contents as free from any dependence or servitude. On the Continent, where classical scholars were wont to distinguish between their philological and their linguistic pursuits, 'linguistics' was, until Saussure and long after the publication of his *Cours*,[1] largely identified with comparative grammar, and, accordingly, the difference between the former and the present status of 'linguistics' is the more striking.

Yet this newly won autonomy is frequently lost sight of, since many linguists are prone to stress, less the unity and recent self-sufficiency of their discipline, than its multifarious connexions with other branches of research, old and new, humanistic or scientific, such as psychology, logic, anthropology, cybernetics, and electronics. This, of course, mainly results from the fact that, in the scientific world of today, few linguists are just linguists and nothing else. Just as, in the past, a linguist was necessarily a philologist and, more often than not, the student of some literature, he is now likely to be an anthropological linguist, a mathematical linguist, a statistical linguist or, of course, still, a philological linguist. Plain linguists are few and far between. Being one of them, I may perhaps be excused for concentrating on language as my sole subject, limiting my excursions outside of that domain

[1] Now available in English: *Course in General Linguistics*, transl. by Wade Baskin (New York, 1959).

to cases where they may be conducive to a better understanding of my own field.

It is not by chance that the establishment of general linguistics, i.e. the study of language for its own sake, coincided with the proclamation of the view that the study and analysis of *états de langue* should necessarily precede any other linguistic endeavour. Language had, until that time, been mainly considered in its evolution, and, accordingly no one had tried to conceive of it outside the context of ever-changing human needs that, at all times, jeopardize the balance of its economy and lead to the restoration of that balance in a new form.[1] At one time identified with logic or reason, language had, by many, been viewed as a product of collective thinking and was consequently placed at the intersection of psychology and sociology. That double dependence accounted for its perpetual instability, nay, made of this instability one of the basic features of language and thereby hopelessly blurred the boundaries between language, as we conceive of it today, and what acts upon it from the outside. Only the strictly synchronic approach recommended by Saussure could lead to the foundation of an autonomous science of language through a drastic severance of all its ties with physical and psychic reality.

Decades of effort toward perfectly static descriptions, culminating with Hjelmslev's purely formal analysis,[2] have failed to convince us that they represent an ideal starting-point for linguistic research. But without Saussure's figment of the transversal cut,[3] the perfect autonomy of linguistics might still be a long way off. To that figment we owe the conception of a linguistic structure perfectly distinct from the

---

[1] On language economy, see George K. Zipf, *Human Behavior and the Principle of Least Effort* (Cambridge, Mass., 1949), pp. 19–22, and André Martinet, *Économie des changements phonétiques* (henceforth *Économie*) (Berne, 1955), pp. 94–97, and *Éléments de linguistique générale* (henceforth *Éléments*) (Paris, 1960), pp. 182–7.

[2] See *Prolegomena to a Theory of Language*, transl. by Francis J. Whitfield (Suppl. to *IJAL*, vol. 19, no. 1) (Baltimore, 1953).

[3] *Course*, pp. 87–88.

physiological, psychological, and sociological factors which, at all times, prepare, out of the language of today, the language of tomorrow.

No wonder 'structure' has become the rallying sign of contemporary descriptivists. It points, of course, to a coherence of the components, but, at the same time, to the aloofness of the whole from all the rest. 'Function', which is quite fashionable in some quarters, has no great appeal in linguistics. It is obviously redolent of the uses to which languages are put; it suggests contacts with the world at large, those very contacts we have had to disregard in order to achieve self-sufficiency. Yet, since we are all agreed that language works as an instrument towards certain goals, we can hardly deny that the functioning of that instrument should be one of our major concerns. Actually, all 'structuralists' reckon with the function of linguistic units: setting apart a feature as 'distinctive' implies that its function suffices to make it an object of interest and assign it to a definite class. But becoming conscious of the paramount importance of function in linguistics will normally lead to a greater respect for reality. And what is meant here by 'reality', is not any physical or semantic trait which happens to be singled out, but linguistic reality, that which is recognized as such because it belongs to a given language where it exerts a definite function. Function supplies the linguist with a scale of values that will stubbornly resist any attempt on the part of the theorist to make facts submit to the requirements of a method. Function may help in bridging the gulf between the so-called progressive and traditional groups. It may bring about contacts that will dispel, on the one side, the belief that only sluggishness and vested interests are preventing one's opponents from discovering the truth, on the other side, the conviction that the new trends are incompatible with careful observation and respect for facts.

The most deeply rooted objection to 'structuralism' is, indeed, that concentration on 'structure', whatever that may be, will necessarily lead scholars away from a close scrutiny of observable facts and make them disregard whatever stands in the way of their attempts to set up theoretical constructions. In fact, no one among those acquainted with the linguistic practice of the last decades would deny that there is some truth here. We all remember so-called descriptions in which, at every point, facts were culled from the most various sources, without any regard for consistency, so as to make them fit the author's preconceptions. Should this be structuralism, no serious scholar would want to be a structuralist. But, even if we leave aside that sort of irresponsible juggling, it cannot be denied that any effort towards establishing a single method for the treatment of all linguistic facts or the description of any language whatever, will, almost inescapably, result in giving the same status to things which differ, not only physically—which would be quite in order—, but also in their role in the economy of the language.

Language reality is far more varied and far less homogeneous than many descriptivists would be willing to concede. At many points it gradually merges into other aspects of reality, which explains why it has taken such a long time to secure the autonomy of linguistics. For a linguist who is, above all, intent upon not jeopardizing this painfully achieved autonomy, the normal reaction to a situation where the limits between language and non-language seem to be blurred is to proceed arbitrarily and draw clear-cut distinctions even across uncertain ground. Once his domain is thus delimited, he may proceed to submit all its parts to one and the same treatment. Yet he may, all the time, be painfully aware of the fact that this type of procedure will more or less distort the picture he will be drawing. From this he may conclude that there is no such thing as 'structure' in language itself, that what is so called is nothing but a frame invented by the linguist in order to help him to classify the data. In other words, a structuralist is not one who discovers struc-

----

[1] Cf. W. S. Allen, *On the Linguistic Study of Languages* (Cambridge, 1957), p. 14.

tures, but one who makes them.[1] This is, of course, an extreme attitude, but it clarifies the more average position according to which the actual existence of structure is, at least, not postulated.

This highly formalistic approach underlies the practice of a probable majority of contemporary descriptivists, although it is professed only by a handful of theorists for whom consistency is a fundamental requirement.

The realistic conception of linguistic structure as a feature of linguistic reality is apt to be mistaken for the naïve assumption that all that is physically present in speech is part of that reality, irrespective of whether it has a function and what that function is. Actually, structure can be found in language only, as it were, as an aspect of its functioning. The varieties of function establish among data a hierarchy which involves distinguishing between cores and margins, for whose description different methods have to be used. Function is the criterion of linguistic reality. Our duty is to describe that reality, and it should be no cause of alarm if one of our operational devices is found to fail us at a certain point. These devices, such as phonemes, for instance, do correspond to definite aspects of linguistic reality as shown by the speakers' comportment, and we value them in so far as they do, but no further.

We need not be ashamed of presenting marginalities as such in our descriptions, because they are the proof of the latter's truthfulness. Natural scientists, who approach their own problems far more soberly than do our theorists, are well aware of marginalities in those aspects of the universe it is their duty to investigate and to describe. Zoologists, for instance, have gone on registering all phenomena as they entered the field of their observation and have never tried to do away with the platypus. Why cannot those who study man's behaviour become reconciled to its entire range?

Our first illustrations will be borrowed from the field of phonology.

According to the phoneme theory, every utterance, in any language, is totally analysable into a succession of distinctive units; these units are discrete, and their number, in the language, is strictly determined. Methods have been devised for the analysis of utterances into phonematic segments. It is clear, for instance, that the Spanish word *mucho* is made up of four successive phonemes: the segment corresponding to the *ch* group of the spelling is one and the same phoneme, although it begins as a stop [t] and ends as a fricative [š], because that fricative never occurs in Castilian Spanish without the preceding stop, which implies that this stop, as such, is automatic and not distinctive. The reasons for conceiving of the consonantal complex at the beginning of English *chip* as a single phoneme are undoubtedly very cogent, although not quite as obvious as in the case of Spanish *ch*. But there are many cases on record where no agreement has ever been reached as to whether one should reckon with one phoneme or two successive phonemes: some would analyse the word *ice* into two, others, into three phonemes. If *ice* presents two phonematic segments, an /ai/ phoneme has to be listed among the phonological units of the language; this will probably entail a similar decision regarding /au/ as the former of the two segments of *out*. If, on the contrary, *ice* is made up of three segments, *out* follows suit and English loses two phonemes.[1]

Faced with such a problem, the formalist will reach an arbitrary decision. But since he wants to be consistent, he will formulate his verdict so that it can be used as a precedent if some similar case arises. This, however, should not be construed as if he were looking in the data themselves for a justification of his comportment.

The realist may also have to decide on one interpretation or the other, because of some practical necessity, such as the

[1] Contrast Trubetzkoy's position in *Grundzüge der Phonologie* (Prague, 1939), pp. 108–9, with the average Bloomfieldian analytic approach as, for example, in George L. Trager and Henry L. Smith, Jr., *An Outline of English Structure* (Norman, 1951), pp. 19–22.

requirement of a subsequent statistical study. But he will explain the reason for his choice, and stress for the reader the factual impossibility of equating, say, the case of /ai/ with that of a clear-cut phonematic duality, as in the case of /kl/ in *clear*, and a clear-cut phonematic unity, as in the case of the first vowel of *father*.

If the analysis of utterances into a number of successive phonematic segments raises some questions whose solution is not quite obvious, the next phonological step, namely the identification as one phoneme of segments appearing in different contexts, is so full of epistemological pitfalls that most structuralists prefer to sidetrack the problem altogether by declaring that phonetic likeness should be the only guide. This, of course, sounds beautifully sensible and is, in practice, highly satisfactory until one comes across cases where a sound appearing in a given context seems to stand just half-way between two of the sounds that are attested elsewhere. Here again, some arbitrary decision is inescapable, unless one is ready to restate the problem in functional terms: is the distinction that generally obtains preserved or not in the position at stake? At this point, the rank and file of Bloomfieldians will shudder and exorcize the spectre of the archiphoneme by pronouncing the magic formula: 'once a phoneme, always a phoneme!'

If we now come back to reality, we soon discern that while no one can question the fact that there is between *big* and *beg* a difference, lying somewhere in the middle of the two utterances, which suffices to distinguish them, it is far more risky to state that the two vowels of *kitchen* are the same. For a satisfactory functioning of the language, at any rate, it is essential that the vowel of *big* and that of *beg* should be kept distinct, but it is immaterial whether the two vowels of *kitchen* should be the same, or not the same at all. In theory, there is no reason for the system of word initial consonants to present any point of similarity with that of intervocalic or word-final consonants. We could easily imagine a language where all word initials would be articulated in the front part of the mouth, and all the final consonants at the back and in the throat, so that it would be meaningless to try to pair every unit of one system with one of the other. What prevents this is, of course, economy: people who make distinctive use of labial stop articulation in one position would be stubborn monsters if they resisted, throughout millennia, its extension to other positions.

Where economy requires that systems of distinctive units *should* differ from one position to another, systems *are* different, as is shown by the coexistence of vocalic and consonantal systems.

It is quite essential to try to understand why we all insist on calling the [p] of *pat* and that of *tap* one and the same phoneme. We do so for no cogent theoretical and abstract reason, but only because both appear to be the product of the same muscular habit with just the necessary adaptations imposed by the respective contexts. Both are prevented from drifting by the same inhibitions determined by the necessity of keeping them distinct from other articulatory habits, the same ones for the [p] of *pat* and that of *tap*. If the competing articulatory habits were not the same for initial [p] and final [p], if, for instance, the language under consideration were not English, where we have *tab* alongside *tap*, but one, like German or Russian, where no such pair could be found, some of the drift-preventing inhibitions existing initially would be found missing finally. Strange as it may sound, true realists, in such a case, would object to the complete identification of initial [p] and final [p] even if these could be shown to be physically identical. What is decisive, in language, is achieving communication, and this is secured if, at every point in the utterance, the unit chosen is kept distinct from the ones that could have been used, in the very same context, in order to make a different message. But how close this unit is to one actually used elsewhere is of secondary importance. It is quite obvious that we are trained, from infancy onward, to detect in the speech of others what corresponds to distinct choices on their part. Learning to speak is learning to make the choices current in one's community.[1] Phonemes are such choices. They do play their distinctive role precisely because they are specific choices and recognized as such.

It is at the same time normal that there should be different systems for vowels and for consonants and that the various consonantal or vocalic systems of a given language should tend to present similar distinctions, but no one should try to spirit away any discrepancy between the distinctive pattern in one position and that in another. Yet formalists have rationalized some of their arbitrary decisions into a principle of simplicity, according to which the best language description is the one which presents the fewest possible units. When they come across a situation where one type of distinction is found in position A and another type in position B, they never stop before they have convinced themselves, if not others, that the two types are nothing but avatars of the same distinction.

The case of French /ɛ/ affords a nice illustration of formalistic and realistic practice in a case of that sort: Parisian speakers of my generation are apt to distinguish between *un mètre*, 'a metre', and *un maître*, 'a master';[2] the distinction lies in the vowels: both are normally said to be [ɛ], with or without minor tamber variations, the difference being one of duration or whatever gives that impression. In word-final checked syllables, such as *mètre*, *maître*, the only other front retracted vowel units are /i/ as in *mitre*, 'mitre', and /a/ as in *quatre*, 'four', which gives a partial system that could be represented as follows:

$$/i/ \; (m)itre \quad \begin{array}{l} /ɛ/ \; (m)ètre \\ /ɛ̄/ \; (m)aître \end{array} \quad /a/ \; (qu)atre$$

[1] Cf. *Éléments*, pp. 31–32.

[2] Cf. André Martinet, *La Prononciation du français contemporain* (henceforth *Prononciation*) (Paris, 1945), pp. 126–9; the distinction is being abandoned, as shown in Ruth Reichstein's 'Étude des variations sociales et géographiques des faits linguistiques', *Word*, xvi (1960), p. 61.

In absolute final position, the same French usage distinguishes four vocalic qualities, /i/ as in *riz*, /e/ as in *ré*, /ɛ/ as in *rais*, /a/ as in *rat*. Here, the partial system looks as follows:

$$/i/ \; riz \quad /e/ \; ré \quad /ɛ/ \; rais \quad /a/ \; rat$$

We have thus four distinct units in both positions, and the principle of simplicity will convince formalists that the final /e/ of *ré* must, by hook or by crook, be identified with either one of the two /ɛ/'s of *mètre* and *maître*. Pure and conscious formalism will favour an arbitrary solution. Mitigated formalism will try to buttress its decision by reference to minor tamber variations. After long hesitations, Roman Jakobson decided in favour of equating the vowel of *ré* with the short /ɛ/ of *mètre*, whereas the long vowel of *maître* was identified with the /ɛ/ of *rais* whose duration, in the dialect being discussed, is the normal short one of word-final vowels.[1] Should instrumental observation reveal, in many speakers, a slightly closer vowel in *mètre* than in *maître*, this would certainly not point to any tendency to make it conform with the close vowel of *ré*, because if such a tendency existed it is hard to see why it should not be more successful.

Instead of looking from one local system or inventory to another, we shall, more realistically, consider what happens in a definite position, namely before word-final -*tre*, where vocalic phonemes have, of course, to be kept distinct from one another if linguistic communication is to be secured. Next to our two /ɛ/'s, in the system, we find two [a] phonemes, those of *quatre* and *pâtre*; the former is often said to be front and the latter back, and here lie the essentials of the distinction in strictly local Parisian pronunciation where the vowel of *pâtre* might, in the 1920's, have sounded like the

---

[1] The present writer was used as a native informant, and his testimony was solicited first in favour of the identification of the vowel of *ré* with that of *maître*, then in support of the grouping which was eventually retained in R. Jakobson and John Lotz, 'Notes on the French Phonemic Pattern', *Word*, v (1949), p. 154.

-aw of English *law*.[1] In another type of pronunciation, which has greater prestige, the tamber difference is much smaller, and it is eked out by a difference in length, so that the vowel of *quatre* can be said to be short and front, that of *pâtre* long and slightly back. If we now consider our vowels in the frame of the articulatory quadrilateral, it should be clear that the two short vowels, that of *mètre* and that of *quatre*, are about as distant as the two long vowels, that of *maître* and that of *pâtre*, the former pair lying a little higher and more to the front than the latter, as shown on this diagram:

This is the type of fact on which linguistic realists are likely to capitalize. In the present case, even in a purely static presentation of the vocalic structure of French, their awareness of the importance of the relationships among the units which really form a system, i.e. among which speakers have to choose at each point, if communication is to be secured, will prevent them from ascribing too much importance to the relationships among units from one system to another and indulging in largely arbitrary speculations as to how maximal descriptive simplicity is to be achieved.

The case of what is called the French 'mute *e*'[2] gives a more dramatic illustration of the contrast between what I am tempted to call formalistic totalitarianism and realistic discrimination. English spelling is full of silent *e*'s, as in *case*, *mute*, and *give*. Since they never correspond to any audible articulation, they do not raise any phonological problems. In French, some *e*'s are found in the spelling where, according to context or style, either nothing is heard, or a more or less centralized vowel is sounded, which we will henceforth designate as [ə]. It is important to notice that such an alternation of zero and [ə] is never found initially in an utterance or

[1] Cf. A. Martinet, 'C'est jeuli le Mareuc', *Romance Philology*, xi (1958), p. 352.　　　　[2] Cf. *Prononciation*, pp. 37–70.

a word, but always after a consonant. In normal everyday unsophisticated spoken Parisian French, the alternation of zero and [ə] is in ninety-nine cases out of a hundred automatically regulated by the context, and this irrespective of whether some *e* appears in the spelling or not. Phoneticians usually say that the appearance of the [ə] vowel is regulated by the 'law of three consonants',[1] which prescribes that [ə] should be pronounced where it will prevent clusters of more than two consonants, thus, for instance, in *arquebuse* and *contre-maître*, where it finds its expression in the spelling, and in *ours blanc* [ursəblã], and *arc-boutant* [arkəbutã] where it does not. This amounts to saying that 'mute *e*' is no phoneme since its appearance is automatically determined by the context, and that for every consonant phoneme of French we should reckon with two allophones: a purely consonantal one, the one we find for /d/ in *dans*, and one, partially vocalized, which we encounter in *devant* ([dəvã], phonemically /dvã/).

All this is, of course, a greatly simplified picture of reality: there actually are cases in which the pronouncing or not of 'mute *e*' may make a difference in the interpretation of what is said.

First of all, French children in the course of their slow and protracted learning of a difficult language, eventually manage to distinguish between two different treatments of words beginning with a vowel, the one which prevails in the enormous majority of cases and which children tend to make universal, and the other which is reserved to words which used to be pronounced with initial [h]. Hence *l'eau* [lo], but *le haut* [ləo], *l'être* [lɛtr], *un être* [œ̃nɛtr], but *le hêtre* [ləɛtr], *un hêtre* [œ̃ɛtr]. As is shown by some of these examples, the phonic difference often lies in the presence or absence of the so-called 'mute *e*'. This implies that [ə] cannot be equated with zero before a word-initial vowel.

The name of the ram, in the medieval epic of Reynard the Fox, was *Belin*, and this survives as a surname, but in two

[1] Maurice Grammont, *La Prononciation française*, 7th ed. (Paris, 1930), p. 105.

different forms, *Blin* and *Belin* which are phonemically quite distinct: some people are called *Blin* and others *Belin*, and confusions are not likely. With ordinary nouns, which are normally preceded by an article, the situation is different, and I have heard children wonder why a small fish (*l'ablette*) had the same name as the weasel (*la belette*).

At the age of six, children go to school and begin to learn fables and other pieces of verse. Now, French metrics are based upon the language as it was pronounced at the beginning of the sixteenth century when all 'mute *e*'s' were sounded or, at least, made a difference, unless they were elided. A line like

Et je sais que de moi tu médis l'an passé

which would amount to ten syllables in normal speech ([ɛʒ-sɛk-də-mwa-ty-me-di-lã-pa-se]) is recited with the regular twelve syllables of the alexandrine. This contact with classical poetry is, with the average child, too incidental for him to learn where to put a 'mute *e*' and where not to put it. What he remembers is that one has a right to insert a 'mute *e*' after any consonant if metric necessities require extra syllables. And this is indeed what happens when children sing their own words to a tune; as, for instance, *On t'emmène ce soire* . . . instead of the traditional *Va chez la voisine*. . . . In popular poetry, the 'mute *e*'s' of the spelling are sounded or not, according to the occasional needs of the author. A protracted contact with classical verse will, however, finally condition people in that respect. Apart from the initial consonant, I pronounce *soir* and *poire* alike; but I would no longer accept them as rhymes.

The above is a realistic sketch of a most intricate problem. It is realistic because it indicates certain aspects of the linguistic comportment of French speakers without trying to account for them all within one and the same formula. A totalitarian approach would consist in stating that since there are cases when [ə] instead of zero makes a difference,

/ə/ is a phoneme and should be marked as such whenever it is actually or potentially there. 'Potentially', of course, is meant to take care of traditional poetic diction. This type of description, if it deserves to be called a description, has definite practical advantages: it gives the language a monolithic appearance which is thought, in many quarters, to make the approach to French as a second language easier; it meets with the approval of the mass of educated Frenchmen who are inclined to identify culture with the written form of their classical heritage; but its main advantage in the eyes of the formalist consists in the vistas it opens toward a further simplification of the pattern: it is clear, for instance, that if we can analyse *cane*, 'duck', which is pronounced [kan], as /kanə/, nothing but phonetic reality (but who cares about that?) can prevent us from analysing *quand*, which is pronounced [kã], as /kan/, and in general analysing nasal vowels into oral vowel plus nasal consonant. We thus get rid of the four distinctive units we would have otherwise to posit in *vent*, *vin*, *long*, and *un*. It is true that a word like *canton* will thereby require six successive phonemes (/kanton/) instead of four (/kãtõ/).[1] But it would seem that formalistic simplicity applies exclusively to the number of units in the system, not to that in the utterance.

The main disadvantage of this type of interpretation is that it gives a completely distorted picture of present-day natives' linguistic comportment. Toward the end of the fifteenth century, French was a language in which, with very few exceptions, all syllables ended in a vowel, very much like the Old Macedonian of Cyril and Method.[2] Consonantal groups were unpronounceable unless they existed word-initially: in a word like *absent*, the *b* must have been mute in normal speech. On the other hand, [ə] was the only vowel found in totally unstressed position, and consequently it could be dispensed with without any resulting confusions. Through

---

[1] Cf. Knud Togeby, *Structure immanente de la langue française* (*Travaux du Cercle Linguistique de Copenhague* 6), 1951, p. 58.   [2] Cf. *Économie*, pp. 326–8, 349–52.

this gradual elimination of [ə] wherever the result was not too heavy a cluster, biconsonantal groups of all kinds became pronounceable: *gibecière*, 'satchel', formerly a four-syllable word, was reduced to two with the group /bs/ in between. From that time on, speakers could yield to the suggestion of the spelling and sound the -*b*- in *absent*. Therefore, the /-bs-/ cluster in *absent* is not, in ordinary speech, different from the same group in *gibecière*.

From an educational standpoint, it may suffice to state that no one can hope to understand spoken French before, consciously or unconsciously, he has learned to disregard 'mute *e*' as a distinctive segment except in the very specific situations which have been noted. It is not our purpose, here, to examine how this could be achieved.

A last illustration will also be borrowed from French, but this time I shall consider the case of a grammatical category, namely gender. Here is a difficult problem which we can only hope to clarify if we refuse to let ourselves be rushed into accepting from the start a totalitarian approach.

My choice of French is largely determined by the fact that, since there are only two genders in that language, it will be easier to conceive of the gender system in its totality, if indeed we are entitled to speak of it as a system. It goes without saying that the conclusion at which we shall arrive regarding French does not necessarily apply to other languages, even those as closely akin as Italian or Spanish.

French distinguishes between a 'masculine gender' and a 'feminine gender'. The formal behaviour of nouns belonging to the masculine gender is simpler. If all nouns behaved like them, there would, of course, be no gender problem, quite exactly no gender. We may therefore assume that the feminine gender is the key to gender. We might have done the reverse and considered normal the behaviour of feminine gender nouns: then, the masculine gender would have been the key to the gender problem. But our actual choice is operationally preferable.

First, it is essential to distinguish feminine gender from reference to female sex: when English speakers say *she*, instead of *he* or *it*, it is because they intend to refer to a female being or, exceptionally, to some machine they choose to consider in the same relation as a female. The language offers three possibilities. The speaker is determined to choose one or another by non-linguistic factors. On the contrary, when French speakers say *elle* instead of *il*, they do so because they cannot do otherwise. Apart from highly exceptional cases which we shall see later, there is, in such a case, no trace of a choice on the part of one who pronounces *elle*. The speaker is forced to use this or that pronoun because he is referring to a linguistic unit that requires him to say *elle* instead of *il*. If, as I believe we should, we refuse to identify as a linguistic unit a segment that does not correspond to a new choice of the speaker, we must declare that gender in French is no morpheme. The situation is perfectly clear when, leaving aside the personal pronoun, we concentrate on the marks of gender in the nominal group. When I say *la grande montagne blanche*, I choose to use the definite article and not the indefinite *une*; I choose to qualify the mountain as great; I choose to speak of a mountain and not, for example, of a curtain; I choose to qualify it as white. But I never choose feminine instead of masculine. This does not mean that I refuse to characterize the mountain as a female: I certainly do. It means that I am not given a chance to choose a gender, because as soon as I say, or foresee I am going to say, *montagne*, I cannot avoid giving the definite article and the accompanying adjectives the fuller, so-called 'feminine', form. My choice of *montagne* implies a number of formal accidents which tradition labels as feminine forms. In Saussurian terms, we may say that the *signifiant* of the feminine noun *montagne* is not limited to that form, but that it is discontinuous and emerges at other points of the utterance. In our particular instance, it shows as the / . . . a/ of *la*, the /. . . d/ of *grande*, the / . . . ʃ/ of *blanche*.

Gender is quite frequently lumped together with number, as two frequent nominal categories. But this should not induce us to put them on the same level of analysis. Number, the plural number, for instance, is, in French, a morpheme: if instead of *la montagne* /lamõtañ/, I say *les montagnes* /lemõtañ/, I choose to say /... e .../ instead of /... a .../ because I want to stress that several mountains are involved, not one. Nothing, in the context, compelled me to say *les* instead of *la*. The plural was a new choice.

It might be argued that French adjectives are frequently used by themselves, both the masculine and the feminine forms, with the power and function of a noun, and that, in such a case, the marks of the feminine stand by themselves without the support of the feminine noun. But, of course, the adjective, here, is in the feminine because it refers to a substantive which is understood, and could be furnished on request. In most cases of that kind, we would find the substantive to be actually present if we cared to include the whole conversation in the context, so that here again the feminine would not correspond to a new choice.

All this might induce us to state that the class of feminine substantives in French is nothing but a group of nouns which share certain formal characteristics. Theoretically, the case would not be different from, say, that of the English substantives ending in *-ow*, such as *shadow, widow, morrow*, which have nothing in common except that final *-ow*. Of course, the *significants* of French feminine are discontinuous and their elements are dependent on the choice of accompanying adjectives, whereas the *-ow* of *shadow* can never be separated from *shad-* and is quite independent of the surroundings. But once these purely external features are set aside, the contents of the feminine gender boil down to zero, French feminines having hardly more in common than English *-ow* substantives have.

Other circumstances have to be taken into consideration, however, before we may venture to draw our conclusions:

it must be kept in mind that when a formally feminine noun is applied to some animate being, that being is normally a female. There are, of course, a good many exceptions: *baleine* 'whale' is a feminine, which does not imply that the French believe whales are exclusively females. Still, the feminine gender of *baleine* cannot be equated with that of *chaise* or *table*. When referring in English to a chair or a table, I, a native speaker of French, am not tempted to use *she*. But, in reference to a whale, *she* would naturally be on the tip of my tongue. For the French, the unicorn is a female for the purely formal reason that *unicorne* was interpreted as *une icorne* before becoming *une licorne*. Consequently, it is difficult for me to get reconciled to hearing, as I recently did in a film, a unicorn referred to as *he*. There is at least some hint of sex in the feminine gender when used in reference to what has a sex.

Furthermore, we should not disregard the fact that the feminine form of many adjectives differs from the corresponding masculine in exactly the same way as the designation of the female differs from that of the male: formally, *belle* is to *beau* what *chamelle* 'she-camel' is to *chameau*. Jocularly, one could and does derive from *bourreau*, 'hangman', a word *bourelle* for a 'she-hangman'—or should I say 'a hangwoman'? We really cannot argue that we have, here, a pure and simple case of homonymy, because both uses of the *-eau/-elle* alternations actually fade into each other as shown, for instance, by the substantival uses of *beau* and *belle*.

Last but not least, *elle* is sometimes used in reference to females who, in the same context, have been designated by means of a masculine noun. A female physician is normally referred to as *un docteur*, but this never entails the use of the masculine personal pronoun *il*. In a sentence like *Le docteur est arrivé; elle est dans le salon*, there is no doubt that the pronoun refers to the sex of the person and not to the gender of its nominal designation. However, it is worth noting that, in the case of male beings designated by means of feminine

nouns, the grammatical concord is preserved: *la sentinelle . . .
elle. . . .* The use of *il* in such a case would imply that the
specific reference to the soldier as a sentinel had been forgotten. It would seem that the lack of gender agreement in
the case of *le docteur . . . elle . . .* is a recent development and
can still be considered a strictly marginal affair. But it points
to the fact that the use of *elle* instead of *il* may be governed
by non-linguistic factors, and this is a first step on the road
followed by *she* in the course of the history of the English
language.

A totalitarian description of the French language would
capitalize on this still sporadic phenomenon, stress the formal
identities in the expression of sex and gender, and finally
emerge with all the features of the traditional, highly
idealistic, presentation of grammatical gender where it was
assumed that the exhaustive distribution of all concepts into
two classes of masculines and feminines entailed the anima-
tion and sexualization of all conceivable objects.

A discriminating and functional approach will, of course,
stress the actual lack of function in a large majority of cases,
namely when the substantive, whose gender entails some
formal modification of articles and adjectives, is present
among them. It will take into consideration the somewhat
'pronominal' value gender marks will assume when the
substantive is understood or remote in the utterance, and it
will take care of occasional lacks of gender agreement. But no
formulation shall be striven for, which, in an effort to cover at
once all known facts, would infallibly blur and even conceal
the most specific, enduring, and characteristic features of
gender.

It might be tempting, at this point, to indulge in a simile
and say that a formalistic description is to the language what
a geographic projection is to the actual shape of the con-
tinents, in the sense that the centre of the map is fairly
accurate, but the margins are distorted, sometimes beyond

recognition. But this would give too flattering a picture of the achievements of formalistic linguistics. What really happens, in too many cases, is that the inclusion of margins warps the whole description in their favour at the expense of what is, linguistically, really vital, as when the basic non-distinctiveness of 'mute *e*' in French is never even mentioned because all centres around the exceptional cases where it assumes a distinctive function.

The danger inherent in the attempts to squeeze all facts, central or marginal, into the same pattern exists on all planes of linguistic description. It lurks, from the start, in attempts to define the object of our science. In theory at least, the first question a linguist should ask and try to answer is: What is language? We may, in true Saussurian fashion, come to the provisional conclusion that language is a system of signs. But, of course, the question arises whether all systems of signs are languages. Offhand, honest and sedate linguists, who are trained to operate on such languages as Latin, Russian, Chinese, but hardly on traffic signals, are inclined to give a negative answer; but faced with the complexities of human languages, with central cores and marginalities that they dare not identify as such, they finally yield to the pressure of 'annexationists', those who want to put the language label on as big a chunk of semiology as they can grasp. This leaves us without a definition of what it is our duty and our aim to investigate, namely human language properly so called in its different forms, the languages as actually spoken by men.

If we want to know what language is, we should not try to list all the features we may have come across when studying the most diverse languages, and draft a definition which will somehow vindicate them all. We should rather try to determine what all the languages we know, all the communicative instruments we want to call 'languages', really have in common, so that we would not be willing to call 'language' some semiotic system which did not present that minimum.

Languages serve many purposes. They certainly help us to think. They give us an outlet for our pent-up feelings. We use them as artistic mediums. But they are first and foremost used for communication, i.e. transmission of experience from one person to another. Communication is, of course, involved in the artistic uses we make of language, and what is not communication there belongs to expression, a phrase which, in technical parlance, we should reserve to self-centred linguistic activity which does not aim at transferring information from speaker to hearer, but to give the former relief from internal pressures and tensions of all sorts. Soliloquy, which is pure expression, is normally frowned upon as unsocial behaviour, and those who want to 'express' themselves, will have to cheat and procure a victim with whom they can sham communication. This explains why linguistic evolution is entirely determined by the communicative needs of man: soliloquy, if it were not aping communication, would soon result in the annihilation of language.

It may not be out of place to mention here that when I speak of experience as being transmitted by means of language, I give these terms their broadest possible meaning: experiencing a wish or a craving is part of experience, and its transmission may assume various forms: plain statement, request, or command.

Experience as such, prior to all attempts to transmit it to others, is not couched in words, except, of course, if it is gained through linguistic communication. A very immediate type of experience, such as pain, is a good starting-point for understanding how and at what point language enters the picture. Vocal reaction to pain may be purely reflex: a groan. The groan may also be willed and meant as communication, but it is no linguistic communication: cats do communicate with their meows, yet we do not want to include meows in language. Language begins when the homogeneous unanalysed feeling is interpreted into a succession of definite vocal stretches, each of which can be used in the transmission of totally different types of experience, but which, when grouped and ordered as we hear them, convey fairly specific information about what the speaker feels. Should I say, for instance, *I have a headache*, I would use five vocal stretches, namely *I*, *have*, *a*, *head*, and *ache*, each of which can be found in totally different contexts for the conveying of entirely different things; they are thus most unspecific, but, when grouped, they reach a fairly high degree of specificity.

It is not too clear what is meant when laymen describe human languages as 'articulate'. It is likely that people who use this phrase just repeat what they have heard without having ever thought of the implication of that term. Yet it describes perfectly what characterizes human language, less in contradistinction to various forms of animal communication than in contrast with human experience before it has been analysed with a view to linguistic communication. What characterizes linguistic communication and opposes it to prelinguistic groans is precisely this analysis into a number of units which, because of their vocal nature, are to be presented successively in a linear fashion. These are the units which many contemporary linguists call 'morphemes'. But in view of the fact that a number of others use 'morpheme' for different purposes, I prefer calling them 'monemes'. Monemes are the smallest segments of speech that have some meaning attached to them. According to Saussurian terminology, they are minimal 'signs', with two faces: *signifiant* and *signifié*.

The way experience is analysed differs from one language to another. The set of habits we call a language suggests the breaking up of experience into a number of elements for which the language in question has equivalents: a language may use, for headache, a specific moneme, something like *migraine*, instead of two. Where the English say *lift*, others would speak of a *hoisting machine*. The way people proclaim their ignorance is very differently articulated in English *I don't know*, in French *je ne sais pas*, in German *ich weiss es nicht*. But differences in articulation show not only in the way monemes are combined into utterances, but also in the range of choices people have at every point: where an English speaker may choose among *blue*, *green*, and *grey* for conveying his experience, a Welshman will have to be content with a single colour designation *glas*. All this points to a fundamental feature of human language: its variation from one community to another and its variation through time. Throughout the world, cats say *meow* because this results from voice accompanied by a lazy opening and closure of the jaw. Language varies because it suits the varying needs of man. It follows that any feature of speech that is automatically found in all communities must be considered non-linguistic or, at best, marginally so. It is not a matter for the linguist to deal with, but for the psychologist, the physiologist, or both, since these scholars study man in general, assumed to be the same throughout mankind. Our aim, once we have agreed on the features we want to find in an object before we list it among languages, is to describe languages, i.e. to indicate what makes a given language different from all others, whether these are actually described, known to exist, or just conceivable. The necessity of taking into consideration languages unknown to us compels us to reckon with all the possibilities that are not explicitly or implicitly ruled out by our definition of language.

The articulation of experience into successive units is only one of the two features which we want to include in our definition of language. We have to reckon in language with a second articulation, that of the phonic aspect of every moneme into a succession of distinctive units, the phonemes. Every one of the five units of our former example is formally made up of one, two, or three sounds or phonic complexes, to which, as such, no meaning is attached, but whose choice and order fully characterize the moneme whose manifestation they are: *head*, for instance, is made up of the three phonemes /h/, /e/, and /d/ in this order.

Linguists of the old school, Saussurians included, might be tempted to forget or disregard the second articulation. They would thereby miss some fundamental conditionings of human communication. The obvious advantage of the second articulation is economy. The first articulation was economical in the sense that with a few thousands of fairly unspecific monemes, it was possible to shape an infinity of different communications. In the same way, the second articulation is economical, since the judicious combination of a few dozen phonemes enables man to keep distinct all the monemes he needs. In view of the great variety and richness of human communication, the double articulation was bound to be a feature of human language: let us try to imagine how we would fare if we, both as speakers and hearers, had to distinguish the thousands of homogeneous grunts which we would need for every one of our monemes if the second articulation were unknown. It is clear that the lexical expansion made necessary by the progress of mankind would have been unthinkable without the tremendous economy entailed by the breaking up of *signifiants* into phonemes. But there is more to it than economy. If the form of every moneme was an unanalysable grunt, there would be a complete solidarity between sense and vocal form. Meaning would exert a direct influence on form, and form on meaning, the result being that at every instant, every speaker would be tempted to adapt his pronunciation to the particular shades of meaning he would want to convey to his audience. As a final result, both form and meaning would be in a permanent state of wavering, and this would prevent the establishment of discrete meaningful units, what the monemes of our languages actually are thanks to their well-defined and stable forms. The articulation of *signifiants* into a succession of phonemes practically excludes the meaning of a given word from exerting any influence on its specific form. There exists a solidarity among all the performances of the same phoneme which tends to preserve its identity whatever the sense of the word may be. The phonic environments may result in distortions or warpings away from the performance of the phoneme in isolation. But the semantic context is normally powerless. All this is, of course, nothing but a synchronic version of the regularity of phonetic changes: only in very particular cases, which should be especially accounted for, may meaning affect phonetic evolution. This phonematic solidarity can only be explained if we conceive of the phoneme as an articulatory habit, something we should always keep in mind, even if we choose to disregard it temporarily when concentrating on descriptive methodology.

A problem which always arises when language is to be defined is whether the vocal nature of speech should or should not be included in the definition. On the one hand, it is a fact that the languages linguists deal with are or were primarily spoken, even when we can only approach them indirectly through written texts, and that, for a deeper understanding of those written texts, we should always try to imagine the spoken medium upon which the written literary form was based. On the other hand, written language has a structure of its own, the study of which comes within the realm of the linguist's preoccupations, and including the term 'vocal' in the definition of language might be interpreted as unduly narrowing the field by excluding areas where linguists feel perfectly competent. Besides, some scholars always want to grab the largest possible share of the epistemological cake. Yet, there is one important argument in favour of including vocal nature in our definition, namely that vocal quality is directly responsible for the linearity of speech and the consequent linearity of script. It is clear that if signs were visual and presented on a surface, there would be no need for language to be manifested by a succession of items: the painter who is presenting his message on canvas must necessarily delineate his figures one after another, but the recipient of the message may collect it in any order he chooses, casting a general glance or concentrating on particular features as he sees fit. Should the message be *the man is killing a bear*, the onlooker might easily grasp it at first sight, whereas the hearer will perceive it successively. The history of writing begins with painting, i.e. a type of message which is completely independent of language and speech, and leads through stages to alphabetic writing which implies complete conformity to the double articulation of language. But writing becomes distinct from painting as soon as objects and figures are shifted ever so little from the respective positions which they would be expected to occupy in space, in order to suggest a succession reminiscent of the one our language units have in speech. It is true that we could easily imagine some other code, a gesture code or, why not?, an olfactory code which would also impose successiveness. But it is hard to imagine all the implications the particular nature of various bearers of meaning would have had for man's communication. The vocal nature of human language is certainly no peripheral aspect of it, but a basic feature, without which linguistic organization might be fundamentally different from what we know it to be.

All of this points to a definition of 'language' which might run as follows: A language is a medium of communication according to which human experience is analysed, differently in each community, into units (monemes) with a semantic content and a phonic shape. This phonic shape, in its turn, is articulated in distinctive and successive units (phonemes) whose number in a given language is fixed and whose nature and mutual relations also vary from language to language.

This means that we should reserve the term 'language' for a medium of communication which is doubly articulated and whose outward manifestation is vocal. Apart from this common core, nothing can be said to be linguistic which cannot differ from one language to another. This is how we should understand Saussure's dictum that linguistic features are arbitrary or conventional.

It is clear that this formulation, in spite of its unwieldy length, does not list all the types of features that may enter the fabric of language. We may even be sure that it does not include elements which probably play some role in all known languages. There is no mention anywhere of speech melody, which, in the minds of some educators, should embody the most salient features and decisive aspects of the language they teach. We might dispose of an objection coming from those quarters by arguing that the vocal nature of speech, covered in our definition by the word 'phonic', implies the use of the so-called organs of speech, among which are the vocal chords; the vocal chords necessarily vibrate at a certain musical height, and the melodic continuum that results from a continuous vibration of the glottis is precisely what we referred to as speech melody, a physical reality some people hastily identify with intonation. We shall revert to this later. We should first answer another objection which affords a very welcome illustration of the divergences between the formalistic approach to linguistics and the one which I would recommend. I must say, at once, that I do not remember having heard it formulated, except perhaps by myself. In any case, there is enough of a formalist left in me to anticipate it. It is not true that any utterance can be analysed into a neat succession of monemes, each with its own nicely wrapped-up meaning and clear-cut segment. When I say *he cut*, where is my segment corresponding to the meaning 'past'? In French *elle va au marché*, with *au* a single phoneme /o/, what slice should I ascribe to my preposition and what slice to my definite article? As regards our second articulation, we have seen before how difficult it is to analyse into phonematic segments words like *ice* and *out*, and I have suggested that our failure may reflect less the imperfection of our methods than a factual indeterminacy.

Our answer will be that we have not said, or implied, that the whole of language, as represented by corresponding speech, could be exhaustively reduced to successions of monemes and phonemes. We have said simply that what we want to call a language makes use of monemes and phonemes; whether it adds to them other tricks which may at times blur or distort some features of double articulation is another matter.

If we consider double articulation as the core of language, and would see in the rest just margins, it is because this removes language farthest from indiscriminate, unanalysed, interjectional, prehuman, or, should we say, proto-human, forms of communication. This alone can secure for language the stability and rigour that result from the use of discrete units. We all, at one time or another, may get impatient with double articulation because some intonation or some interjection will enable us to achieve what we want far more quickly and at a much lower cost. But this means nothing more than the observation that it often consumes more time and energy to get someone to do something through asking him than through giving him a push. Using language is a very complex and abstract procedure which is well adapted to a certain degree of sophistication, but which, in a number of trivial circumstances, may economically be replaced by some more direct means of communication such as gesturing, either with the hands or the shoulders, or with the glottis. In which case, if the use of language is concomitant, we speak of intonation.

The advantage of calling intonation 'gesturing' is that it removes it at once to the far periphery of the field of language. But of course no one will accept this, except perhaps as a metaphor, like the *Lautgebärden* of a former generation of psycho-linguists. A gesture properly so called may be accompanied by noise, a snapping of fingers, for instance, but it cannot be sheer noise. Only a convinced functionalist could accept the view that a noise is not first and foremost a noise. Since intonation is produced by the vocal chords, and since the vocal chords are *par excellence* the organs of speech, intonation cannot be anything but speech. This dictum sounds very much like common sense, and although I, for one, am convinced of its fallacy, I will not reject intonation from linguistics. It can, indeed, be made to play a role similar to that of monemes, in such close co-operation with the most central and abstract of linguistic tools that any linguistic description would present wide gaps if all reference to intonation were to be avoided.

Actually, no clarity can be achieved in our discipline without establishing some sort of functional hierarchy. We shall, no doubt, have to state that some feature or some aspect of speech is *not* linguistic: this will be said, for instance, of the initial rise of a speech melodic curve; this rise is due to the fact that the glottis, starting from a state of rest, will have to reach some degree of tension, and that the speaker is not likely to wait until that degree is reached. Yet we shall have to distinguish different levels of linguistic relevancy: some French speakers pronounce their *r*'s as a tongue-tip trill, others as a dorsal fricative. This is found in Germany, Holland, and in some other linguistic communities. But it is far from universal. It is a culturally conditioned trait, not an inescapable result of the working of man's psychic and physiological make-up. It has no function, if we reserve this term to cases where some choice of the speaker is involved. It may, however, inform the hearer about the origin, urban or rural, of the speaker and, consequently, colour his interpretation of the message. Some mention of all this must be included in a description of French or German, and how could we totally deny the epithet 'linguistic' to something which it is the duty of the linguist to describe?

The double-articulation theory and any definition of language based upon it leaves a wide margin, for which the name 'prosody' is today a widespread designation. Anything may be said to be prosodic that does not fit in the monematic and phonematic segmentation; so that the American 'suprasegmental' is not a bad substitute. I just think nothing is gained by speaking of 'suprasegmental phonemes'.

It must, in any case, be kept in mind that some prosodic features like intonational contours are not distinctive in the sense in which a phoneme is distinctive, but directly meaningful: a rising interrogative contour on *you like it?* has about the same function as the *do* of the more traditional *do you like it?* In other words, it might be equated with a moneme, not with a phoneme. In Saussurian terms, it is a sign, a minimal sign, with a *signifiant*, the melodic rise, and a *signifié*, 'interrogation'.

The distinction should thus theoretically be made between double articulation and prosody and not, as is traditional, between phonematics and prosody. Yet this latter practice is in many respects amply justified because it is very exceptional to find as clear-cut a *signifié* as the one corresponding to the rising interrogative contour, intonation generally lacking the discreteness of many gestures. If we consequently agree to lump together phonematics and prosody under phonology, we must point out that the distinction between the two branches of phonology is based on differences in segmentation, and that this dichotomy may at times conflict with the classification based on function.[1] For instance, tones, or as some people call them tonemes, have exactly the same function as phonemes: they are distinctive, which means that the speaker, at a certain point in the message, will have to choose between a number of them in order to say just what he wants to say. It is, of course, perfectly immaterial whether the choice is conscious or not. If tones are not considered distinctive features of vocalic phonemes, it is because they are usually found to affect, not a vowel phoneme as such, but a syllabic nucleus, often made up of two or more phonemes or even more than one syllable. This is shown by Swedish or Norwegian, where the distinction between the two tones requires at least two syllables to be preserved: *kòmma* 'comma'

---

[1] Regarding the methodological conflict between segmentation and function, cf. A. Martinet, 'Accent et tons', *Miscellanea Phonetica*, ii (London, 1954), pp. 13–14, and *Éléments*, pp. 54–57.

and *kŏmma* 'come'. In a language where syllabic nuclei always coincide with vocalic phonemes, considering tones as distinctive vocalic features, together with degree of aperture, lip-retraction, or nasality, might not be objectionable. But where this is not the case, we have to separate tones and phonemes, although they function alike, and put the former with accent and whatever remains of the melodic curves when tones have been extracted.

We should, of course, by no means define the domain of prosody by reference to the physical nature of the features we want to include: should, for instance, nasality prove supraseg-mental, we should not exclude it from prosody on the ground that it normally appears as a phonematic characteristic; in many languages a glottal stop or catch functions as a tone and is regularly regarded as such although the glottal stop is, in many languages, a phoneme, just like /h/, another glottal product. It is, however, interesting to notice that the features which are normally made use of in prosody are those that are necessarily present in all utterances: stress, for instance, conceived of as the degree of energy with which a spoken stretch is articulated, is always there; as soon as voice is heard, the vibrations of the glottis must have a given frequency, which results in melodic height; duration is, of course, unavoidable in speech, since speech exists through time. It is therefore understandable why speakers rarely get a chance to oppose these features to their absence at a certain point in the utterance, but only to choose between their modalities, which may vary from one part of the utterance to another. Consequently, they are not so well adapted to characterizing discrete units as others, like, for instance, nasality or dorsal occlusion, which may or may not appear in a given utterance: if I say *What shall we do today?* I make no distinctive use of either of these features, while I cannot help giving my utterance a duration, using a varying amount of energy from the first to the last phoneme, and whenever voice is there—and voice must be there—giving a certain frequency to my glottal vibrations. The needs of communication, acting on pre-existing, traditional linguistic patterns, may yield strange results which seem to challenge articulatory and acoustic economy, as when, for instance, a language with a series of glottalized consonants extends it to the labial position, in spite of the fact that this involves using the cheeks, which are the worst possible organs to use when what is at stake is securing in the mouth as high a pressure as possible. In general, however, language economy will tend to eliminate such quirks and to restrict the play of the different organs to those to which they are best adapted; this accounts for the preference evinced for stress, pitch, and duration in the prosodic domain, and their limited employment outside of it. Within prosody, however, pitch features seem to be well adapted to a number of different functions, and there is perhaps no better illustration of how the same physical fact can be used linguistically for totally different purposes than a precise functional analysis of speech melody.

We should remember, first of all, that speech melody cannot be left out, because voice is a normal ingredient of speech, and voice cannot exist without pitch. Before speech begins, organs are normally at rest, and some time will elapse before they reach the degree of tension found to be normal for a certain style. This accounts for the normal pitch rise at the beginning of an utterance. Voiceless stretches, usually very short, within an utterance do not seem to affect the general tension of the glottis. When the end of the utterance is getting near, the speaker will tend to anticipate it and allow the organs to relax before speaking stops altogether. This accounts for the speech drop at the end of utterances whenever there is no reason to check it. But it must be kept in mind that, whereas the initial rise is physiologically determined and consequently fairly stubborn, the final drop can easily be replaced by some other contour. This being the general conditioning, it is easy to see how variations of that curve can be put to use in human communication:

a drop is interpreted as the end. This being no discrete unit, the lower the drop, the more final the statement will sound. It cannot be said that a rapid and deep fall 'means' contempt, but it is normally indicative of some such feeling in the speaker, or, at least, since everybody knows how to play the game, it is what the speaker wants his audience to believe. The less abrupt the fall, the friendlier it will sound. The frequency of statements with level final contour in polite British usage bears witness to an unmistakable effort not to give offence. The least indication of a final rise will suggest non-finality. The interrogative final rise is just one type of those non-final contours. Within the unit of utterance itself, the sentence, a slight rise will normally precede any pause, since otherwise a pause might be interpreted as the end of the sentence. In Ghiliak, there is a speech segment with the sound [ɸuru] with no specific function except the support of a melodic rise which might be interpreted as follows: 'the preceding pitch fall indicates the end of a sentence, but the present rise indicates that it is not the end of the story yet; please, don't clap your hands'.[1] French political oratory makes use of a similar trick: the gasping orator, who does not want to be interrupted by applause, lets his voice sink towards the end of the period, but immediately tags the first word of his next sentence with a rising pitch, which will secure him the breathing spell he needs.

The picture we have just drawn of the main features of speech melody is not, as it might seem, exclusively derived from a narrow, personal experience, but is, at least, buttressed by recorded observation. Nevertheless, it cannot be assumed that no language ever shows deviations from this general pattern. In sketching it, we have not included the possibility that some stretch of the melodic curve might be needed for the marking of a distinction, as is frequently the case in so-called tone languages; we have disregarded the

[1] This illustration is taken from the material collected in Japan by my colleague Robert Austerlitz.

fact that word accents may also affect the form of that curve; we have left out of the picture the existence in many, and perhaps all, communities of favoured contours which may entail, on the part of the users, a slightly different interpretation of other contours. We mean this pattern to be nothing but a point of reference, which should prevent describers from forgetting how much in speech melody is conditioned by human physiology and psychology and consequently is not and should not be the concern of the linguist.

The first task of the linguist in prosodic matters is obviously to spot in the melodic curve all the stretches that have functions, in other words, the tones or tonemes. Once they have been identified and classified, they should be abstracted from the curve. Whether what is left, after they have been disregarded as so many accidents, can be identified with the above-mentioned pattern seems to depend on the importance of tone distinction for the language, and the complexity of the tonal pattern: in African languages with two tones, a high one and a low one, the tonal succession does not seem to blur the general melodic pattern, so that the latter may be relied upon to indicate whether the utterance is a statement or a question: 'high' and 'low' mean above and below what the general direction of the curve would lead one to expect if it were not for distinctive tones. In Vietnamese, on the contrary, where a six-tone system is the norm, with a high and a low register, with one rising, one punctual, and one interrupted tone for each, it is doubtful whether enough freedom is left to speakers in melodic matters for them to make use of the latitude offered by the general pattern.

If the language under description is not a tone language, the describer will have to determine whether the language makes use of an accent, and, if it does, how accentual prominence is indicated and whether and how it affects speech melody. Recent investigations seem to indicate that pitch plays a much more decisive role in accentual matters than had previously been assumed for such a language as English.

It would seem that an essential ingredient of English accent, traditionally but perhaps mistakenly called 'stress', is a sudden and rapid rise . . . or fall of the pitch.[1] In any case, accent is likely to modify the normal course of speech melody, and such accidents as it may cause in it will have to be abstracted, just as tonal accidents were. A common error consists in ascribing to a vast ill-defined domain of intonation a number of features which functionally belong to that of accent. The use of 'stress', which refers to a physical reality, instead of 'accent' is apt to confuse even competent scholars and make them speak of intonation as soon as they fancy they are hearing pitch instead of stress: for many of them, the difference between *to increase* and *an increase* would be due to a different placing of stress, while that between *a móving van* (a van used for moving furniture) and a *moving ván* (a van in motion) results from the use of a different intonational contour. Once accent is defined, not in reference to an alleged physical nature, but as prominence given to one syllable per word, or accentual unit, with a view to marking the respective importance of the units within the utterance, it becomes clear that the difference between *móving van* and *moving ván* is accentual and nothing else.

What we should call intonation is therefore what remains of the melodic curve of speech once all tonal and accentual features have been extracted, and, as rightly pointed out by many scholars, most of what is of interest there centres around final contours. It has become usual to analyse these contours by reference to three or four levels. No one will object to such a practice if those levels are presented and used as a frame of reference with about the same value and function as the vowel quadrilateral of Daniel Jones, with its cardinal vowels in relation to which a given vocalic sound can be characterized. If, however, those levels are meant to be phonemes, there is bound to be some disagreement. It is,

[1] Cf. Dwight L. Bolinger, 'A Theory of Pitch Accent in English', *Word*, xiv (1958), pp. 109–49.

of course, perfectly true that if one of the levels is replaced
by some other, the meaning of the utterance may be changed,
just as the meaning of *I make* is changed if I replace *m* by *t*.
But, of course, *m* and *t* are phonemes because interchanging
them modifies the identity of the moneme where this takes
place, and, thus, the utterance is affected by this interchange
only indirectly through the replacement of one moneme
by another. Our problem here is whether a shift of intonational level is to be equated with the replacement of one
phoneme by another or that of one moneme by another.
Let us assume, for instance, that in a contour describable in
terms of the succession of levels 2–3–2, level 3 is replaced by
level 1. A peak of the curve will then be replaced by a trough.
Level 3, which, all by itself, implied a rise, will be replaced
by level 1, which, all by itself too, implies a dip. This shows
that every one of the relevant successive levels is indicative
of one of the specific directions assumed by the melodic
curve. Now, each of these successive directions is contribut-
ing something to the significance of the total contour. This
contribution is additive, as is the one of a moneme to the
meaning of an utterance. It is not destructive, as that of
a phoneme whose presence signalizes that any inference, as
to the meaning of the utterance, which might be drawn
from the context considered without it is wrong: if, to the
statement *it is good*, I add *very*, I am just adding some additional information without deleting what was previously
there, but, if to the statement *it is a roe* I add a /d/ phoneme,
the statement becomes *it is a road*; one element of information
roe is deleted and replaced by another one. Since a level is
just a way of indicating a direction, and since every successive direction would seem to add something to the whole, it
is permissible to state that the value one may wish to ascribe
to a given contour does not actually go beyond the values
that might be attributed to every one of its successive levels.
In other words, inasmuch as the contour has a bearing upon
the sense of the message, it does so as the sum total of the

implications contributed by every one of its components, the levels. This amounts to saying that the relation of levels to contour is comparable with that of words to sentence, in which both words and sentence are signs with *signifié* and *signifiant*, and basically different from that between phoneme and word, or moneme. Should we insist on identifying the items we operate with in intonational matters, with the units that are the frame of double articulation, we would have to say that levels are monemes, i.e. minimal units with meaning, whereas contours are a succession of monemes. But I do not think anything is gained through confusing the different planes whose distinction has proved instrumental in clarifying the working of language.

The central problem of intonation, a problem which, having hardly been formulated, has, to my knowledge, never been tackled, is that of the relation between the levels as posited by the language describer, and their linguistic reality, or, in other words, the behaviour of speakers. It seems clear that they are not discrete units because it is never quite immaterial for the message whether the 'level' is performed a little higher or a little lower; a level implying bitterness or contempt will be the more bitter or contemptuous if it is pronounced a little lower than may be usual; with phonemes, which are typically discrete, the precise way a phoneme is pronounced cannot change the message: *dab* remains 'dab' and nothing else, whatever the amount of voicing of its initial /d/, as long as there is enough of it to keep *dab* distinct from *tab*. But, if intonational levels are not discrete, do they or do they not, in a given language, correspond to some habitual comportments? If they do, it means that a certain type of situation normally entails the choice of a certain level, which, as we have seen, determines a certain direction of the melodic curve. If this is the case, any perceptible deviation from this direction must be considered and classified as an individual deviation from a norm. It is a meaningful variation, but still a variant of a type. The answer to this query could only be obtained through a mass of instrumental recordings submitted to a statistical examination. This, of course, would have to be done for a large number of the most diverse languages before a well-founded general linguistic treatment could be presented.

That such intonational habits exist need not be further substantiated. They are some of the features that often enable people to state that some person has this or that 'accent'. But it remains to be determined how far such habits actually hamper or prevent individual uses of the natural implications of speech melody.

What, in any case, is perfectly obvious even before any world-wide research programme has been carried through, is the linguistically marginal nature of intonation, which should be obvious as soon as a dispassionate examination has deprived this term of its glamour and limited its application to some residual uses of speech melody. This, to be sure, is very much the same as to give your dog a bad name and hang it. But need we care what terms we use, provided the analysis is correct and fruitful?

II

TOWARDS A FUNCTIONAL SYNTAX

IF asked about the history of structural linguistics, most people concerned would probably say that it all began with the phoneme. When structuralists chose first to concentrate on what we have called the second articulation, they certainly found the correct approach towards greater rigour in the treatment of linguistic problems: the discrete nature of linguistic units is ultimately based upon the discreteness of the phoneme, and phonology was the foundation we needed for any further progress. Still, dealing so long with phonemes before attacking the more intricate field of the first articulation had an unfortunate consequence: having achieved outstanding success in 'phonemics', linguists were legitimately induced, when tackling the actually far more complex study of the significant aspect of language, to use a similar pattern. This accounts for frequent terminological pairings such as *phoneme–morpheme*, *phone–morph*, *allophone–allomorph*, and so forth, and, on a different level of abstraction, the isomorphism of the glossematicians with its strict parallelism of the two planes of expression and contents.[1]

The most fundamental objection to this practice of identifying the patterns on two different planes derives from the obvious fact that, in language, something which is not manifest, variously called meaning or experience, is manifested by means of something else. This, no doubt, implies a one-to-one equivalence, that of the *signifiant* and the *signifié*, but not necessarily an identical behaviour of the minimal, significant unit, which I call the moneme, and of the minimal distinctive unit, the phoneme. The moneme is

---

[1] Cf. Jerzy Kuryłowicz, 'La Notion de l'isomorphisme', *Recherches structurales* (*Travaux du Cercle Linguistique de Copenhague* 5), 1949, pp. 48–60.

a Saussurian sign, a unit with a meaning and a phonic shape, i.e. one which combines something that is not manifest with its outward manifestation. It belongs to the two planes of expression and contents, and it is the smallest segment that does. The phoneme has a phonic shape, but no meaning. It is pure manifestation and belongs exclusively to the plane of expression. The moneme-and-phoneme approach to linguistic analysis—and, for that matter, the widespread morpheme-and-phoneme one too—does not coincide in the least with the two-plane pattern of glossematics: considering an utterance like *give me the book*, glossematicians will put, on one side, the individual 'cenemes' like /g/, /ɪ/, /v/, the *signifiants*, either minimal (/gɪv/, /mi/) or complex (/gɪv mi ðə bʊk/), and their graphic equivalents (*g, give, give me the book*) as well; on the other side the *signifiés*, either minimal ('give') or complex ('give me the book'). The basic glossematic dichotomy can be represented as follows:

$$
\left.\begin{array}{l} \text{/g/} \\ \text{/gɪv/} \\ \text{/gɪv mi ðə bʊk/} \end{array}\right\} \sim \left\{\begin{array}{l} \text{'give'} \\ \text{'give me the book'} \end{array}\right.
$$

Linguists, who, explicitly or implicitly, operate according to the double-articulation pattern, will keep their phonemes alone, and put *signifiants* and *signifiés* together according to the following schema:

$$
\text{/g/} \left.\right\} \sim \left\{\begin{array}{l} \text{/gɪv/—'give'} \\ \text{/gɪv mi ðə bʊk/—'give me the book'} \end{array}\right.
$$

This lopsided diagram conveniently illustrates how the moneme stands on a far higher level of complexity than the phoneme and why any effort towards pairing them is bound to result in distortion.

The fundamental difference between distinctive and significant units must ultimately account for one very important discrepancy in the syntactic comportment of phonemes and monemes: a phoneme fulfils a function in a definite position. If we want to identify a *signifiant*, e.g. that of the word *lake*, it is not enough to say that it is made up of three phonemes /l/, /e^i/, and /k/ because the same phonemes are those which characterize the words *clay* and *kale*; one must specify: /l/, /e^i/, and /k/ in that order. In other words, when pronouncing *lake*, speakers have to choose, in initial position, /l/ and oppose any inclination to say /k/ for *cake*, /t/ for *take*, &c. Postponing /l/ till the end of the word and anticipating the choice of /k/ would not do, because we would thus get *kale* which is not what we mean. All this, which sounds trivial, is, in fact, basic for the establishment of the phonematic pattern of the language.

The situation is different with monemes or significant elements generally; the relevancy of order is far from general: it is fairly immaterial whether I say *the one I like is Paul* or *Paul is the one I like*; the implications are different if I say *with Paul, I went to Rome* and *I went to Rome with Paul*, but they do not affect the identification of the moneme group *with Paul*, and the same applies to *yesterday* in *I went . . . yesterday* and *yesterday, I went. . . .* Certainly, the respective position of monemes is often determined by tradition or by the need to distinguish between utterances with different meanings: it just isn't done to say *Paul with went I Rome to*, and it is far from immaterial whether I speak of *root hair* or *hair root*, not to speak, of course, of the difference between *the man kills the bear* and *the bear kills the man*. But it is clear that whereas phoneme classes can be established by listing all the phonemes that appear in a given context, this cannot be done indiscriminately with monemes, and it might seem that the first step with them should be to determine the situations where their presence results from an exclusive choice, as is normal with phonemes.

It is, however, preferable by far to forget the phonemes for a while and try to discern what comportment we may expect

on the part of monemes as the products of the first articulation of language. Let us start again from the experience that
has to be communicated. If the communication is to be
linguistic, that experience will have to be analysed into a
number of elements for each of which the language under
consideration has an equivalent, a moneme with its meaning
and its phonic form. For simplicity's sake we shall assume
at this point that the phonic form of every moneme is always
neatly circumscribed. The communication will thus take the
form of a succession of monemes, each corresponding to some
definite element of experience. But, of course, the choice and
nature of the elements of experience will vary from one
language to another. Let us suppose that the experience to be
conveyed could be rendered in English by means of *Yesterday,
there was a riot in the village*. One of the elements of the English
analysis is the moneme *riot*; *riot* applies to a definite happening, and it is immaterial whether it has previously been
identified or not: a riot in English is always *riot*, whether
it is *a* riot or *the* riot; many languages do not bother about
distinguishing between previously mentioned and not
previously mentioned; English does, and this specification
is treated as one of the elements of experience; now, we could
imagine a language which would have a different moneme
for 'a riot' and 'the riot', as if people said, for example, *riot*
for 'a riot' and *brawl* for 'the riot'. This would, of course, be
most uneconomical, and when people really care to distinguish between definite and indefinite, they manage to
procure articles which become elements of experience in their
own right. In some languages, the simple mention of a riot
may suffice, in the absence of any restrictive moneme, to
indicate the reality of the riot; in our hypothetical language,
riot might mean not only 'a riot' but also 'there is a riot'.
English, just like a good many other languages, needs an
actualizing phrase (*there was*) which we might be allowed
to consider a single moneme, were it not accompanied by
a moneme indicative of time, in this case past time. This

could, of course, be easily dispensed with in an utterance like the present one, where *yesterday* refers specifically to a well-defined segment of past time. Consequently, *there was a riot*, with its four monemes, is the reflex of a specifically English analysis, into four elements, of one aspect of our experience, where some other language might get along with only one.

Another aspect of our experience is rendered by means of the phrase *in the village*. The moneme *village* represents, as an element of experience, a place, but not necessarily a place where something is happening; *village*, preceded, of course, by some article, as here, could be made to designate the place, or perhaps its inhabitants, as the agent of some action, as in *the village decided* . . ., or as its object, as in *they saw the village*. The function would, in both cases, be indicated by the respective position of the elements. In our present case, the circumstance that the village is the place where something happened is treated as another element of experience whose reflex is the moneme *in*. It would not be difficult to imagine a language in which the moneme designating a village would, at the same time, indicate that the village in question is the portion of space where the experience is located. In such a language, *village* would mean 'in (the) village', and this, of course, all by itself without any case ending, since any case ending would have to be considered the linguistic equivalent of another element of experience.

The third aspect of our experience corresponds to *yesterday*. Were it not for literary and poetic forms such as *yesteryear* and the like, we might consider *yesterday* a single moneme since, in that case, *-day*, as the automatic accompaniment of *yester-*, could not be counted as a separate choice. For our present purposes, we shall take the liberty of disregarding *yesteryear* and congeners and of treating *yesterday* as a minimal unit, just as we would do with German *gestern* or French *hier*. We have thus, in *yesterday*, an exact parallel to what we have just been imagining when we thought of a moneme *village* with the sense of 'place where'; *yesterday*, here, is not the day preceding this day, but that day as the segment of time in which something was happening.

We have been dividing our total experience into three aspects, as we called them, each of which was further analysed into monemes. From a semantic point of view, few people would object to such an analysis. But our semantic reactions are, to a large extent, the reflex of formal distinctions. The formal justification of our initial break up is the fact that our three segments *there was a riot, in the village, yesterday* are syntactically autonomous units: every one of them can be used initially, medially, or finally, without any difference in their own meaning, although, of course, the choice of this or that order may imply some semantic difference for the utterance as a whole. On the contrary, in normal contemporary English, word order is fixed within those segments. The reason for the syntactic freedom enjoyed by those phrases is not far to seek: in every one of them we find an unambiguous marker of its function, i.e. of its relation to the rest of the utterance: *there was* marks *the riot* as the predicate, i.e. as the element around which others gravitate and in relation to which their function will be marked; *in* marks *the village* as indicating the place where the riot occurred; *yesterday*, as such, is the indication of when the riot took place. The relationships between the three main elements of experience are thus precisely indicated, and there is no need here to rely on word order to tell the hearers what these relationships are. A language like Latin extended the practice of explicit function marking to situations where English, and western European languages generally, make use of word order, namely in the indication of subject function and object function. In Latin, a nominal subject was no part of the predicative autonomous phrase, neither was any nominal object: *pater videt puerum* is made up of three autonomous phrases; its English equivalent, *the father sees the child*, is just one, since the respective position of the segments is indicative of their function, i.e. in terms of experience, their relations to one another, which prevents their being shifted at will without changing or impairing the message.

The criterion of syntactic autonomy points to a threefold distinction among monemes: we have first monemes that carry within themselves the indication of their own function and which we shall designate as autonomous monemes: French *vite, hier, demain, dimanche* in *il viendra dimanche*, are autonomous monemes; in English there seem to be few clearly autonomous monemes of that type, but autonomous compounds such as *last night, next week* are at least as frequent as in French, where we have *hier soir, la semaine prochaine*. Notice, in German, autonomous compound numerals such as *neunzehnhundertneununddreissig* with the meaning of 'in 1939'.

Next, we have monemes that do not imply any definite relation to the rest of the utterance and will therefore be available for several different functions. Of course, every one of these functions will have to be indicated somehow, either by position or by means of some additional element. These monemes could be called dependants; *village* is a dependant.

Last, we have monemes which secure autonomy for other monemes to which they are attached, by indicating their function, i.e. their relation to the rest of the utterance. The combination of such a moneme with its dependants is an autonomous phrase. These we shall call functional monemes, functional indicators, or just functionals. Functionals correspond to prepositions and conjunctions of traditional grammar, but also to case endings. The reasons for which people are so reluctant to lump prepositions and case endings together are numerous: first, the former come before and the latter after the form they govern; second, prepositions can be separated from their substantives by various additions such as an article and one or several adjectives, while case endings are permanently glued to the word they characterize; third, there is normally one preposition per phrase, irrespective of how many articles or adjectives are added, whereas case-endings are likely to be found after every one of the additional elements; fourth, in the case of prepositions, the functional usually forms a clear-cut segment of the utterance, in contradistinction to what we find, for instance, in Latin case-endings, where the indication of case, i.e. function, is formally confused with that of a totally different type of moneme, namely number, and where it is not always clear what belongs to the substantive moneme and what to the ending: is the nominative ending of *puppis*, 'poop', *-is* or just *-s* as in *urbs*? All four reasons should not be dismissed as sheer prejudice. But we should never allow them to blur the functional identity of prepositions and cases. All of them are finally reducible to the same phenomenon: monemes, which, for some reason or other, are frequently or constantly in contact and will tend to merge. The merging will be the more likely and the more intimate if the element whose function is indicated comes first, and the functional indicator last. This is due to the fact that, in any language, the number of distinct functions is very much smaller than that of elements capable of performing them; these elements, the so-called lexical items, are more informative and, accordingly, generally given a preferential treatment: they may be provided with an accent which gives them prominence, and their initial phonemes are, as a rule, articulated with particular care so as to facilitate their early identification in the flow of speech.

A formal merging of two or more monemes, I call an amalgam: *he cut*, as contrasted with *he admitted*, can be said to be an amalgam and to result from amalgamation. Fr. *au*, in *au marché*, as contrasted with *à l'* in *à l'hôpital*, is also an amalgam. We may also, if we choose, call *sang*, the preterite of the verb *to sing*, an amalgam, although it is not likely to have resulted from a process of amalgamation. This process is not necessarily carried through so that it becomes impossible to distinguish one *signifiant* from another: in Slavic languages, amalgamating processes have, at different periods, begun to blur the boundaries between the radical moneme *ruk-* 'hand' and following derivational monemes or case-endings; this has resulted in yielding different forms for the radical: in Czech, for instance, *ruk-* in the nominative singular *ruka*, *ruc-* in the locative *ruce*, and *ruč-* in the adjective *ruční*.

Semantic amalgamation is common too, as when *black+mail* becomes *blackmail*. In *window*, or its Danish equivalent *vindue*, originally *wind eye*, amalgamation, both formal and semantic, has resulted in reducing two successive monemes to one. When, as in a form like *blackmail*, the semantic amalgamation is complete, since, synchronically, there is no hope of ever identifying the meaning of *blackmail* as the sum of the meanings of *black* and *mail*, it is certainly advisable to consider *blackmail* a single moneme, because, from a purely synchronic standpoint, the homonymy of *blackmail* and *black+mail* is purely accidental. But when a formal amalgam is still identifiable as limited to a definite formal context, as is the case with Fr. *au* found only before consonants and not before vowels, or when the amalgamated forms combine monemes with perfectly distinct functional values—as with Latin case-endings where, for instance, nominative is a functional indicator, but plural is nothing but a modality of the noun—it is imperative to preserve the distinction. We shall speak then of two different monemes even if an analysis of the form into two successive segments proves arbitrary and, as in the case of Fr. *au*, downright impossible. The Latin form *hominī* conveys three elements of experience: 'man', 'dative', and 'singular'. Should we insist on chopping it up into successive slices, we might rephonemicize it as /hominii/ and say that 'man' corresponds to *homin-*, 'dative' to *-i-*, and 'singular' to *-i*. This analysis might be supported by a comparison with the dative plural *hominibus*, where both *homin-* 'man' and *-i-* 'dative' would reappear, *-bus* being then an 'allomorph of the plural morpheme'. But, of course, *homin-* means 'man' only in combination with a given type of endings, and -ī is the mark of the dative only in combination with certain nouns in the singular. Therefore it is more accurate and, of course, less arbitrary to say that *hominī* means at the same time 'man', 'dative', and 'singular' than to try to segment it. Linguistic articulation may be blurred, and it is our duty to describe it as we find it: we should never try to disentangle formal units which happen to overlap or be confused; yet we should never deny the existence of units, as singular and plural, in Latin,, whose existence is always secured and attested by some formal difference, but in so intricate a fashion as to defy analysis.

Our distinction of three types, autonomous monemes, dependants, and functionals, is based upon syntactic autonomy. But this leaves out one type of moneme or segment which is independent rather than autonomous. Reverting to our former example, we would say that *yesterday* is an autonomous moneme, and *in the village* an autonomous phrase, but *there was a riot* is not only syntactically autonomous, since we can place it initially, medially, or finally at will, but also independent, since we can use it all by itself and obtain a complete utterance, which is not the case with *yesterday*, nor with *in the village*. In our hypothetical language, *riot*, which should mean as much as 'there is a riot', could be used all by itself as a self-sufficient utterance. We would then say it is used with predicative function. The situation, in our English example, is somewhat more complex. *There was a riot* is definitely a predicative phrase characterized as such by what we have called its independence. We took the liberty, in what precedes, of considering *there was* an actualizing phrase and *a riot* the predicate, but others might prefer another kind of analysis and see in *a riot* the subject of the predicate *there was*. This view is supported by the observation that an analysis in terms of subject and predicate seems to be universally applicable in English. Every complete utterance, in that language, centres around a core of two monemes, one of which, as Sapir says,[1] is 'something to talk about', and another which is what 'must be said about this subject of discourse'. Since, in English, the subject is never an autonomous phrase as, for instance, in Latin when a noun, the predicative phrase is always made up of at least a subject and a predicative moneme, whose only possible function is the predicative function, and which we call a verb. The subject, defined as what necessarily accompanies the predicate, is one function of certain classes of monemes which, in the wake of tradition, we could call nominal and pronominal monemes. The other functions assumed by these monemes are those of the so-called complements. In a language where the predicative moneme need not be actualized by means of a nominal moneme endowed with a specific function, we should not speak of a subject. What we would be inclined to label 'subject' because it is rendered by a subject in a translation, is nothing but one of the complements.

We may want to define 'function' as the linguistic counterpart of the relationship between one element of experience and the whole of experience, so that we could speak of function in the case of any one of the marginal elements, but hardly in the case of the predicative core; the predicative function would then be no real function. This, after all, is a matter of convention. But even if we decide to speak of function only in reference to a definite type of relationship, we should be ready to ascribe different functions to the predicate at least in those languages—English is one of them—where speakers have at their disposal two or more forms of the predicate indicating different types of relationships with the participants of the action; if opening is the action, and the participants a gardener and a gate, I may choose to say either *the gardener opens the gate* or *the gate is opened by the gardener*. We will have to distinguish between an active function, and a passive function, these functions being, of course, nothing but our traditional 'voices'. It is not easy to tell what the

---

[1] *Language* (New York, 1921), p. 126.

functional indicators are in *opens* and *is opened*; probably -*s* for one function, *is* . . . *ed* for the other. But, once again, we should not let our analysis be too narrowly determined by the difficulties we may experience in analysing forms.

If we leave out, as a special type, the functions of the predicate, we should distinguish between primary functions and non-primary functions. Primary functions are those of elements which are directly connected with the predicate. In a sentence like *yesterday, the head of the department dictated a four-page letter to the secretary he had just engaged*, the four elements *yesterday, the head of the department, a four-page letter,* and *to a secretary he had just engaged* have some primary function; the function of *the department, four-page, he had just engaged* is not primary, since they are not directly connected with the predicate *dictated*. Within a so-called subordinate clause such as *he had just engaged*, the same functional hierarchy obtains as in the so-called main clause, but we should not speak of a predicate there, but of a 'predicatoid', and the functions of elements directly connected with it should be considered at best primary-like.

Among dependent monemes—those that are neither independent, autonomous, nor function indicators—one should distinguish the ones that assume some primary functions from the ones whose function is not primary. The former could be designated as primary dependents, and the latter as marginal dependents, or determinants; in the above sentence, *head* is a primary dependent, *the* (in *the head*) and *department* are marginal dependents, *the* (in *the department*) is, of course, marginal too, but marginal to the already marginal *department*.

Another possible distinction is that between grammatical and lexical monemes. In order to distinguish between them, one should set up the inventories of the monemes which are found in specific contexts, within autonomous phrases, where the respective position of elements is functionally relevant. Lexical monemes are those which belong to non-limited inventories. Grammatical monemes are those that alternate, in given positions, with a comparatively restricted number of other monemes. The average frequency of grammatical monemes like *of, for, with* or Lat. 'genitive', 'dative', 'ablative' is considerably higher than that of lexical monemes such as *man, rich,* or *eat.* Functionals are grammatical monemes. Among primary dependents some may be lexical (nouns) and some grammatical (pronouns). Some determinants are lexical (an adjective like *great*), and others grammatical (an adjective like *my*, the article *the*, or the 'plural' moneme). Grammatical determinants can be designated as modifiers. Among modifiers should also be listed such grammatical primary dependents as are part of the predicative phrase. These include modes, tenses, aspects, and persons in so far as their *signifiant* is not syntactically autonomous: in *I'll do it, I, 'll,* and *it* are modifiers.

With the setting up of modifiers as a specific type of moneme neatly distinguished from another type of grammatical element we have called functionals, we are definitely breaking with tradition. Stressing, as we have done, the syntactic autonomy of certain units or phrases, is, of course, nothing but pointing out a feature that sets apart adverbs and adverbial phrases in so far as they are used as verbal adjuncts. Labelling predicative monemes as 'independent' does not go far beyond what generations of grammarians have stated about the nature of the predicate. But dividing the mass of grammatical elements into two basically distinct types —the functionals and the modifiers, placing them at two far ends of our chart, and enforcing thereby a strict segregation —may well be felt as verging on scandal. We are so used to listing as belonging together such categories as tense, aspect, mood, and voice, that it may be shocking to hear someone maintain that whereas tense, aspect, and mood are closely akin and belong together, voice is as different from them as different types of monemes can be. We are used to considering gender, number, and case as the three pillars on which any decent nominal system is built, and we may be tempted to resist any suggestion that gender has no separate existence and that number is a local accident of limited importance, whereas case belongs to the constitutive frame of any utterance.

Yet the distinction between functionals and modifiers is fundamental, and it has lately been noticed and pointed out in various quarters.[1] If in a phrase such as *with a smile*, the primary dependent *smile* is considered the centre of the phrase, the grammatical determinant *a* is centripetal, the functional *with* centrifugal: *a* is connected with the rest of the sentence only through *smile*, which it helps to specify; *with* connects *smile* with the rest of the sentence, and since the connexion is thereby established, the speaker is free to place the phrase *with a smile* anywhere he pleases. Syntactic autonomy is thus the criterion which, in all cases, and particularly in formally complex ones, will prove the presence or the absence of a functional. In a context like *the hunter was killing a bear with his spear*, neither *the* nor *a* are functionals, since they do not grant *hunter* or *bear* any syntactic autonomy: exchanging the place of *the hunter* and *a bear* will result in conveying a totally different experience; *with*, on the contrary, makes it possible to place the phrase *with his spear* practically anywhere without changing its relation to the rest of the sentence. Whether this or that functional may or may not be used is partially determined by the communicative needs at that point of the utterance: after *he is distributing tickets*, I may or may not specify *to* whom. But it also depends on which predicative moneme I choose, whether I may or may not use a *to*-complement. It is what is referred to when we say that a given verb governs this or that case. This amounts to saying that, to a large extent, the choice of a functional is predetermined by that of the verb of the clause. On the contrary, the choice of the modifier is free, i.e. the speaker is determined to use *a* or *the*, the plural or the singular, at a certain point by direct

[1] e.g. by Richard S. Pittman, starting with *A Grammar of Tetelcingo* (*Morelos*) *Nahuatl* (Language Diss., No. 50) (Baltimore, 1954), pp. 6–8, and Georges Gougenheim, 'Morphologie et fonctions grammaticales', *Journal de psychologie* (1959), pp. 417–26.

reference to what the experience really is that he wants to communicate. If, in some cases, the range of the choice happens to be limited, it will be so on account of the nature of the unit that is modified, as when a certain noun is never used in the plural, but not because of some limitation imposed by the structure of the sentence as a whole.

In spite of such fundamental differences, functionals and modifiers have so far generally been confused, and it is easy to understand why linguists who, in their overwhelming majority, had been taught Latin grammar first, were tempted, at best, to consider them two aspects of the same linguistic reality. In Latin, as in all Indo-European languages that have preserved the old declensions, the expression of case and that of number are hopelessly mixed under the form of case-endings that resist any formal analysis into successive segments. In other words, amalgams of a functional and one modifier, or more than one, are practically the rule there, and must have been felt by generations of linguists to be a normal feature of any self-respecting language structure. As a matter of fact, it cannot be considered a strange quirk of Indo-European, because amalgams of functionals and modifiers are by no means absent elsewhere. It is quite clear that the *signifiants* of both are likely to appear in close succession in the utterance and are therefore constantly exposed to amalgamation.

But the existence of such amalgams would not suffice to explain the traditional disregard of the difference between centrifugal and centripetal grammatical elements: after all, the existence of complex case-endings never prevented grammarians from distinguishing between case and number. The main reason why the distinction was not made lay in the existence of concord. It was generally believed that the justification for the somewhat clumsy repetitions which characterize this phenomenon was to be found in the way it allowed the speaker to connect the successive elements of the utterance. This was professed even by a scholar like Otto

Jespersen, who had little patience with roundabout ways of
expressing oneself and denounced concord as a most awkward
approach to sentence building. Now, concord which amounts
to using several discontinuous segments for one and the
same *signifié* is attested for functionals and modifiers alike.
This circumstance was, of course, one more reason for identifying them. But what is really basic here is the fact that,
thereby, modifiers would seem to be made to function as
connective elements, a role which we have been denying
them and entrusting exclusively to functionals. The answer
to this is that, if what is normally just a modifier, redundantly
and discontinuously expressed in different positions through
the utterance, happens to act as the sole indicator of a
function, it has to be interpreted, when this is the case, as
an amalgam combining modification of the accompanying
monemes and indication of their relationship to the rest of the
sentence: in a Latin context like *viri vident, viri* contains
a modifier, the 'plural' moneme, and a case, the nominative
which marks its subject function; in *vident* the final *-nt* is
exclusively a part of the *signifiant* of the 'plural' moneme we
have just identified in *viri*. It is worth remarking that the
amalgam of the two monemes 'plural' and 'nominative' is
only partial, since it could be said that the former's *signifiant*
is *-i* . . . *-nt*, while the latter's is just *-i*. But if our subject
belongs to a type where the nominative ending is identical
with the accusative ending, if, for example, our context is
homines animal vident, the *-nt* of *vident* becomes instrumental in
identifying *homines* as a nominative, since it indicates that the
subject is in the plural and, in this context, points to *homines*
as the only form which can be interpreted as a plural subject.
Thus, owing to the ambiguity of the nominal ending, the *-nt*
of the accompanying verb may be made to play the role of the
elements of a discontinuous moneme indicative of the subject function of the neighbouring plural noun. All this may
sound rather tricky, but the facts themselves are so, not our
interpretation, and this is something to which any schoolboy

would readily bear witness. Everything would be simpler if the nominative case were always unambiguously distinguished from the other cases. There would then never be any need to resort to the mark of the plural agreement to indicate which noun is the subject. The intricacies of Latin are no proof that the distinction between functionals and modifiers is not fundamental.

Concord is redundancy, and contrary to what could be expected, redundancy results, as a rule, from least effort: people do not mind repeating if mental effort is thereby reduced; if adjectives are quite freely and frequently used as nouns, as was the case in older Indo-European languages, it will be indispensable for them to carry the mark of their function if nouns do; therefore a word like *fortis*, 'courageous' or 'courageous fellow' is inflected just like *civis*, 'citizen'. If I mean something like 'the citizen, the courageous one', there is some justification in presenting the mark of their function twice, since the two words are more or less equals. But when *fortis* is really nothing but an attribute of *civis*, it would be more logical either to mark it as such, or to use the bare stem, letting its vicinity to *civis* indicate its relation to it. But it is certainly much easier to let the adjectives keep in all cases inflected forms that have had to be memorized anyway. In popular French the equivalent of *my father says* is *mon père il dit* (pronounced [idi]) instead of the traditional *mon père dit*; since I have to use [idi] in reference to my father's saying something when I need not specify that the speaker is my father, why shouldn't I save myself the trouble of choosing between [di] and [idi] depending on whether I expressly mention my father or not? Since I can't help using [idi] at times, it is handier to stick to it, whatever the context, than to reckon every time with the context; pronouncing an extra phoneme is nothing in comparison with the output of mental energy required by the choice between [di] and [idi].

There are situations where it is not usual to speak of concord or agreement, but in which speakers also have recourse to redundancy for obvious reasons of economy: in our former *Yesterday, there was a riot*, the notion of 'past' is expressed twice, once precisely, in *yesterday*, and then rather vaguely, in the preterite *was*. Now, it may be useful to have at one's disposal, together with a set of references to some definite periods of the past, such as *yesterday* or *last week*, some means of labelling the experience as a past one without any further specification. Of course, if we start with a precise reference such as *yesterday*, there is no need to add a vague reference to the past as the one included in *was*. The lazy solution, however, consists in letting the context, *yesterday*, determine the choice of the tense. In similar cases, one might easily be tempted to characterize the tense moneme of *was* as relational, since it sluggishly establishes some connexion between different parts of the utterance. In a similar way, it could be argued that such a modifier as the definite article implies some relation with what precedes, since it normally labels its noun as something previously mentioned. Such facts are what Sapir probably had in mind when he labelled all grammatical items as relational.[1]

It has now become clear that redundancy, grammatical-ized or just lexical, is a basic feature of human communica-tion, and it may in particular instances be resorted to in order to indicate the function of some segment. But, once the uses of the respective positions of monemes have been dis-counted, only such elements as secure syntactic autonomy are to be considered functional indicators. Whether this syntactic autonomy is frequently or exceptionally made use of is immaterial. Even if it could only be shown by means of some unidiomatic syntactic shift, it still would have to be deemed valid, if it were proved thereby that the identifica-tion of functions is not affected.

Most of the preceding examples were borrowed from English, with a sprinkling from other genetically connected

[1] Op. cit., pp. 86–92.

and structurally similar languages. This might lead readers to believe that our analysis is based upon the observation of a certain type of language and, consequently, that it cannot make any claim to universal validity. But this assumption would not be correct: starting from our definition of language as doubly articulated, we have actually been proceeding in a purely deductive way, and the existing forms we have been quoting and even operating with were never meant as support for the theory, but simply as illustrations of the categories we posited as necessary for the functioning of linguistic communication. What has led us to stress the importance of syntactic autonomy is the realization that this autonomy is the test that a segment of an utterance corresponding to a given element of the experience contains all that is needed for marking its relation to the rest. It is a guarantee that the hearers will be in a position to reverse the process through which the speaker breaks down his previously unanalysed experience into a number of elements for which the language he uses offers equivalents. It would seem that there exist only three ways for the speaker to indicate the relation of a segment to the whole:

First, the linguistic equivalents of the elements of experience may be connected by means of units, in all respects similar to them, which we might consider new elements of experience in their own right: in *John's hat*, *'s* is but a handy way of expressing 'belonging to' which is part of the experience just like 'John' or 'hat'; in the same way as some elements of experience may be represented by prosodic features, the marking of relations may be secured by means of an intonational or accentual feature.

Second, the relation between two elements may be expressed by means of the respective positions of their linguistic equivalents in the speech continuum: in many languages, a subject is marked as such because of its position before the predicate; in *John's hat* the respective position of *John* and *'s* marks *John* as the owner.

Third, the relation of an element to the experience as a whole may be included in the 'meaning' of its linguistic equivalent: *yesterday* corresponds to an element of experience whose relationship to the whole is never in doubt. But, beside such perfectly autonomous segments as *yesterday*, we find cases where the 'meaning' of the moneme may, in certain contexts, imply a given function, as when Russian *stol* 'table', as an inanimate masculine, will tend to be considered a grammatical object, in the absence of any specific indication of that function.

Proceeding in a strictly deductive way, it is our duty to determine as we have just tried to do, what possibilities are afforded by the linear form of speech for the linguistic expression of the various functions corresponding to the relations assumed to exist among the elements of experience. But we have no right to posit the existence of relational universals: offhand, we may be inclined to believe that the *with*-type of relation, or *with*-function, exists in all languages; but observation reveals that, in many languages, the equivalents of *do it with a hammer* and *he came with a friend* make use of different functionals; even in a language like French, where *fais-le avec un marteau* and *il est venu avec un ami* show the same equivalent of *with*, there are so many specific contexts where *avec* does not correspond to *with* that it would not be commendable to equate their respective functions. Even on a more fundamental level, we should be wary of following Sapir when he presents the subject-predicate pair as the necessary basis of linguistic communication.[1] Here again, we have to envisage various possibilities and try to imagine what could constitute a minimal utterance, and how such an utterance could be further expanded.

The first problem that arises in connexion with the minimal utterance is whether we should distinguish between normal utterances, the ones which, in English, involve a subject and a predicate, and curtailed ones such as *over there! the scoundrel!*

[1] Op. cit., p. 126.

fire!, not to speak of monomonematic or polymonematic injunctions such as *go! do! get away! give him a shilling!* Traditional
grammarians do not experience any difficulty in such matters
because it is obvious for them that, once injunctions are set
aside, only subject-predicate cores can be dubbed 'normal'.
But this is precisely what we do not accept, because we want
to consider the possibility of languages using utterances
made of one (predicative) moneme in exactly the same situations where other languages, such as English, cannot dispense
with the complex subject-predicate construction.

It is by reference to our distinction between what is
properly linguistic and what is marginally so[1] that we may
hope to give a sound foundation to the concept of 'normal
utterance'. What we consider properly linguistic is what
is achieved, in matters of communication, by means of the
double articulation pattern: double articulation is what pro-
tects the linguistic frame against interference from outside,
what makes it really independent and self-contained. But
communication by means of double articulation is an expen-
sive procedure which man will tend to avoid when his needs
can be satisfied through the use of simpler, more direct
means, such as gestures, by themselves or supplemented by
speech. Another, very effective, way of reducing the output
of energy involved in communication is to rely on the situation in which the interlocutors are placed: *very nice! pooh-pooh!*
no! make excellent sense all by themselves among people
who look at the same thing or witness the same event. This
reliance on situation is so general that all languages have
developed several classes of monemes whose interpretation
is always dependent on situation. Such are demonstratives
like *this, that,* except when used in reference to context, time
references like *now, yesterday, today, last night* or the 'preterite'
moneme, and personal pronouns like *I* and *you.* The situation
generally makes it so obvious who the second person subject
of imperatives is, that its expression is the exception rather

---

[1] See above, pp. 28–29.

than the rule. All these economical tricks are very welcome in linguistic practice, but they undoubtedly detract from the ideal of human communication, which is self-sufficiency. This ideal finds its expression in out-of-situation uses of language as realized, e.g. in gossip, where the reference is to absent people, in narratives generally, and in literature, where use is seldom made of the actual situation, namely the author at his typewriter and the reader with his printed pages and, in between, the long-drawn processes of editing and composition. It is true that authors do create situations where their characters are found to use, with perfect relevancy, such terms as *I, you, today,* or *this week.* But these situations are actually contexts, and therefore a purely linguistic accompaniment.

It is in reference to out-of-situation uses of language that normal syntax can be defined: normal syntax is that which is attested in such uses, i.e. when communication is achieved by purely linguistic means. This should, of course, not be construed as excluding from normal syntax such segments as *I tell you*: it is clear that *I tell you,* as a syntactic pattern, is identical with *they tell them,* which may contain no reference to situation; in other words, *I tell you* is normal syntax, in spite of the fact that this segment contains references to situation, since it conforms to patterns attested for segments that do not contain such references.

This situation criterion is certainly valid for determining what could be called syntactic normalcy in a language, like English, where it agrees with the consensus of generations of grammarians that syntactically normal utterances contain a subject-predicate phrase. Its application to languages that we suspect do not demand a bimonematic core may not be quite as decisive: there are many languages where a moneme meaning 'rain' (with no possibility of deciding whether verb or noun) is used by itself when the English say *it is raining.* In such an utterance, there is no linguistic reference to any situation; it usually indicates that it is raining here and now, but the 'here and now', corresponding to no linguistic units, are no parts of the communication. Still it could be argued that 'here and now' is included in the meaning of the moneme for 'rain' unless specifically excluded by the addition of some complement like 'yesterday' or 'beyond the hill'. Yet, there is no doubt that languages in which the normal way of saying *it is raining* or *there is a fox* is by means of a single moneme meaning 'rain' and 'fox', deserve not to be classed indiscriminately with languages in which this is not possible. The more so if it can be shown that this mono-monematic utterance may be normally expanded by means of various complements, whereby it is revealed as the potential core of an unlimited syntactic complex '[here comes a] fox' > '[there came a] fox, last year, that was killed'.

Even if the minimal utterance in a language cannot be unambiguously shown to coincide with a single moneme, one should not jump to the conclusion that it must necessarily be one of the subject-predicate type. It is easy to understand why so many languages have made it a rule never to use one moneme by itself: even when centring his attention on the existence of a single being, thing, or process, a speaker will normally not be satisfied with the mere mention of that item, but will be inclined to locate it in time or space, or to connect it with himself or his interlocutors. These additions are often conceived as actualizers, which seems to imply that the moneme by itself is an abstraction whose anchoring in reality can only be achieved by means of some element endowed with just that function. This view is supported by the nature of the subject, which is a moneme, likely to be found elsewhere in a variety of complemental functions, used here as the necessary accompaniment of a predicate, with a function perfectly characterized either by some privileged position as in English, or some functional mark as in Latin. But the fact that some languages make the actualization of the predicate a definite function, does not imply that actualization is, in principle, more than one aspect of the basic linguistic process according to which communication can be made more specific by means of additional elements. A distinction may be made between optional specification and compulsory addition, as of a subject, for which the term 'actualization' could by convention be reserved. But it should be kept in mind that a compulsory subject does not really actualize a predicate more than an optional complement would. There may be languages in which one-moneme utterances cannot be considered normal out-of-situation syntax, but in which the predicate can be actualized by means of any complement, the actualizing function being added to any other function the complement or complements may assume.

Traditionally, the term 'predicate' is defined in reference to the subject-predicate complex and would seem to designate everything in the clause that is not the subject, or some dependent of the subject. Besides, 'predicate' implies some assertion, so that a question or an order would not contain any predicate. If the term is to be retained by contemporary linguistics, we shall want to use it in reference to mono-monematic segments which, by themselves, may constitute a complete, out-of-situation utterance, and also to the same segments when accompanied by various expansions (complements), but independently of them. Within the subject-predicate complex, 'predicate' should, in a similar fashion, apply to any segment that is, jointly with the subject, constitutive of the minimal utterance, thus excluding from it its various complements.

A subject is different from a complement only because it is constitutive of the minimal utterance. Therefore, whenever we speak of a subject we are referring to a linguistic situation in which subject and predicate are both equally indispensable, since our criterion is indispensability, and the problem arises of how we can tell what is the one and what is the other. If our terminology makes any sense, the subject should be the one which should somehow stand closer to the marginal and optional elements of the utterance: in many languages, English among them, subject function can be ascribed to such monemes (nominals) as are found elsewhere to assume the functions of complements; in some, such as Malagasy, monemes with subject function must be marked as previously known or mentioned, which shows them to be informationally marginal. The possibility that some languages do not clearly distinguish between two successive statements and the succession subject + predicate cannot be ruled out.

In languages where actualization is needed but can be achieved by means of any complement, the predicate is obviously the one moneme which is not marked as performing any complement function.

All this, and what could be added about the different levels of complementation, amounts to establishing a hierarchy of syntactic functions. This hierarchy is, no doubt, set up with a view to differences between languages, but it should be clear that, even if it were carried through, it would never account for all the varieties of linguistic structure.

It is quite essential to know all the different functions that characterize a language, but it is equally important to determine for each language, what monemes are qualified to perform this or that function. No language is known to allow every one of its significant units to perform all of the functions it provides. It is even difficult to imagine how such a language would work. If, in such a language, functions should be marked by means of functional indicators, these, being significant units in their own right, should be able to assume the role of functioning elements, and, conversely, all functioning elements would also have the role of functional indicators. But how could speakers make clear that a given moneme is used as a functioning element here, and a functional indicator there, if only the respective position of the monemes in the speech continuum could be relied upon? Many languages are recorded in which the same moneme is used either as a functioning element with the meaning of 'to give' or as a functional indicator with a dative value. But in a language like Vietnamese, where this is the case, not all 'verbs' function as 'prepositions', nor vice versa, and this determines significant contexts that enable the hearer to identify 'give' as a predicate or as a dative function marker. There are languages, and Vietnamese is again a case in point, in which position plays a great role in function marking; the main function here can be labelled 'determination', and this is shown by postposition of the determinant; what looks like a subject-predicate relationship might possibly be interpreted as a case of determination. But if the core A receives two determinants, B and C, how can the hearer know that, in the succession A–B–C, C is not a determinant of the immediately preceding B, but one of A, concomitantly with B? Some marker, segmental or prosodic, will be needed, and there goes our monematic omnivalence!

A language in which all monemes would be of the *yesterday* type, i.e. syntactically autonomous, because the indication of the function is part of the meaning of the term, would be so uneconomical that we may as well rule it out as a practical impossibility. Function being, in such a hypothetical case, diluted in lexical meaning, would, of course, cease to exist as such.

We are thus induced to accept, at least as a pragmatic assumption, the view that there exists in all languages some distinction between monemes as regards the extent to which they may assume the various existing functions. In no language are all monemes used indiscriminately as function-endowed and function-marking. In other words, there is no language without grammar. But once unambiguous function-marking is secured, there is no universally valid reason why any moneme, except one that is specifically a function-marker, should be excluded from any function, whether predicative or non-predicative. Still, specialization is very widespread. Many languages have, for example, a class of adjectival monemes more or less restricted to certain specific functions and which, accordingly, tend to identify meaning and function: *small*, for instance, implies not only 'smallness', but also the function of determination, as in *a small car*, and also in *he is small* if we agree to locate the predication in *is*. It is even more frequent to find that a class of monemes (verbs) is restricted to predicative function, although this does not necessarily imply that only verbs can be predicates. Contrary to what was generally assumed, this is a domain where languages are found to vary and which, in consequence, should play a great role in typological matters.

III

LINGUISTIC TYPOLOGY

WHAT contemporary linguists somewhat pompously
call 'typology' is not basically different from what
a long line of thinkers have attempted to do when
they classified languages, not according to their antecedents
and genealogy, but with respect to their directly observable
characteristics. It is not difficult to understand why so little
has been achieved along these lines to date: for more than
a century, practically all responsible and reputable linguists
were engaged in looking for traces of linguistic kinship, i.e.
for evidence pointing to the fact that different languages were
divergent forms of one and the same older form of speech.
We need not go too far back in time to find and, as far as
I am concerned, to remember a period when attempts to
classify languages on any other basis than genetic relationship were frowned upon as a sheer waste of time and energy.
Let me only mention the fact that the second edition of *Les
Langues du monde*,[1] published as recently as 1952, has retained
genealogy as the well-nigh exclusive principle of classification. This, no doubt an extreme case, obviously results from
lack of information, on the part of the surviving editor,
concerning the mid-century status of descriptive linguistics.
But the well-known reluctance of Meillet for any non-genetic
comparison was perfectly justified at a time when there was
no proof yet that linguistic description could be performed
with as rigorous or more rigorous methods than the ones
available for genetic comparison. Although Sapir's typology,[2]

[1] The first edition, published in 1924 in Paris, was entitled *Les Langues du
monde, par un groupe de linguistes, sous la direction de A. Meillet et Marcel Cohen.*
[2] As Chapter VI ('Types of Linguistic Structures') of his book *Language*
(New York, 1921), pp. 127–56; but it is based upon the analysis presented in
Chapter V of the same book ('Form in Language; Grammatical Concepts'),

published in the early 1920's, deserves our admiration and still must be considered the necessary basis of reference for all typological attempts, we may well understand why so many linguists remained sceptical and why it has never been used.

Our fundamental objection to previous attempts at classification is, of course, that they were bound to be random and intuitive, since so little was really known about the languages which we so glibly labelled isolating, agglutinative, or inflexional. If many linguists are convinced that it is high time to tackle typological problems, it is because they think that we are in a position to give a generally valid description of any language, one which is not biased by the background and previous experience of the describer.[1] Furthermore, they deem that we have at our disposal reliable descriptions of a good many languages, and, last but not least, that we know exactly what we can expect from a language, because we ourselves have decided what we want to call a language.

This does not entail, by any means, that reliable descriptions will give us the clue to the problem of establishing a typology which will be found acceptable by anybody but the one who sets it up. If so little has been done about typology during the last decades, it is because no one knows how to establish a hierarchy among the various items isolated by linguistic analysis. Sapir, it is true, taught us that we should not try to reduce the complexities of a language to a single label.[2] But if we try to do justice to all the features that seem to deserve mention, we may end up, not with what we expected to obtain, namely a number of classes among which

pp. 86–126. J. Greenberg in 'A Quantitative Approach to the Morphological Typology of Language', *IJAL*, xxvi (1960), pp. 178–94, translates Sapir's scheme into currently fashionable jargon.

[1] In this respect, Charles Bazell, *Linguistic Typology, An Inaugural Lecture Delivered on 26 February 1958* (London, 1958), seems unduly pessimistic, particularly in connexion with the phonological level (p. 5); actual descriptions, as distinct from programmatic illustrations of a descriptive method at the expense of a given language, manage to present traits such as every one concerned would agree to consider relevant.   [2] Op. cit., p. 128.

individual languages could be distributed, but with a long list of criteria which, when applied to a language, would probably set it apart from all others. In other words, what we could achieve would be a method for trimming our descriptions to their essentials rather than a handy tool for rapid orientation.

Linguistic analysis yields, for each language, a most complex picture with a list of phonemes, a prosodical pattern, a set of morphological alternations, a grammar which some would still divide into a morphology and a syntax, and a lexicon, a kind of rambling and unstable structure with which linguists do not know too well how to operate. The ideal solution would be to reduce all these aspects to one spectrum. In order to achieve this, we might be willing to sacrifice certain features felt to be of secondary importance. But, even so, it is doubtful whether we could ever succeed: linguists have lately been repeating that a language is a structure, or, maybe, a structure of structures, and if this is true, we should expect to find inner connexions extending from one end of the complex to the other end. This would be true if a language were one of those tools or machines that work with perfect accuracy and without any appreciable delay in transmissions. But this is not the case. As we shall see later,[1] every language retains features which result from its functioning several millennia ago: French *il est, ils sont*, German *er ist, sie sind*, preserve to this day an alternation determined, in Proto-Indo-European, by the accentual pattern that must have characterized the verbal inflexions at a remote stage of that language. Redundancy, a normal and necessary feature of all language, constantly acts as a buffer, retarding reactions to such an extent that it may take thousands of years for all the implications of one push to spread to all parts of the structure.

The question has often been raised, whether there was any solidarity between the phonological pattern of a language

[1] See below, p. 138.

and its grammatical structure. If what is meant thereby is that a change on one of these two planes is likely to have repercussions on the other, there is ample proof that such a solidarity exists: the connexion between umlaut and Germanic morphology is obvious, and umlaut as a phonological shift has resulted in umlaut as a morphological device as used, for instance, for the forming of new plurals. Yet, if it is true that any phonological change may involve some morphological change, it is also true that the nature of the phonological change will not determine the nature of the corresponding morphological change: the confusion of *e* and *a* may, in a given language, entail the confusion of the indicative and the subjunctive; but this is no indication that there should be a natural and permanent connexion between the preservation of *e* and *a* as distinct phonemes and the retention of a distinction between the indicative and the subjunctive. On a strictly synchronic level, it is likely that, while the morphology and the lexicon of a language require the existence of a number of phonological distinctions, what those distinctions actually are is of little or no importance. This amounts to saying that it is hard to imagine how a linguist who knows the phonological pattern of a language could guess what the main features of its grammar are or, vice versa, how, having been told what the grammatical categories of a language are, one could tell what its phonemes must look like. It is clear that if the latter were the case we need not worry about the role phonology should play in our typology, since the essential of it should be deducible from a consideration of the morpho-syntactic categories. In fact, however, phonology will have to be represented in a linguistic typology, unless we decide that what it has to offer has no bearing upon what our typology is meant to elucidate.

It is a fact that those who have tried to classify languages so far have not attempted to make use of phonological criteria, unless they were professional phonologists who, in their turn, were not trying to go beyond phonematic or prosodic patterns. Traditionally, classifiers concentrate on morphological traits: they probably believe a linguistic classification should first and foremost aim at grouping the languages of people who share the same outlook. Now, they deem the phonology of a language to be a matter of chance, and the lexicon to reflect the world as it is. But its morphology, which ultimately governs its syntax, is supposed to mirror the psychic activity of its users. When scholars distinguished among isolating, agglutinative, and inflective languages, they certainly believed they were transcending mere linguistic reality and reaching deeper into the psyches of speakers. Some of them—but should we call them 'scholars'?—even went so far as to connect isolation, agglutination, and inflexion with some fundamental, permanent, and inherited features of different strains of men, as when one of them declared that it was a crime for an inflecting woman to marry an agglutinating man.[1]

All this trend of reasoning is, of course, hopelessly outdated, less because of a weakening of racial prejudice among scientists, than on account of the widespread conviction that language is more than the reflection of the world in the mind of man. There is something we have a right to call linguistic reality which combines *signifié* and *signifiant* and which is distinct from both the phonic and the mental realities. Language is an institution. A language is a set of habits that the child—or the adult in the case of a second language—acquires by imitation of those who surround him. If we want a linguistic typology today, it is certainly not with a view to establishing a hierarchy of human races or discovering distinct varieties of human minds.

This leads to the question: for what purpose do we want a linguistic typology? It would probably be more truly scientific not to consider ulterior motives. At the present time, as applied linguistics gains more and more importance, it is imperative to insist on the necessity of promoting free

[1] Quoted from Sapir, op. cit., p. 131, n. 2.

research with no other aim than the expansion of knowledge. Still, we cannot work here without criteria for determining what is subordinate and what is essential. These criteria cannot be chosen arbitrarily if we want to reach agreement among linguists; they are likely to be generally accepted only if the final result opens new vistas and reveals new fields for research. This means that we should try to determine the possible reasons why two languages which are not genetically related, i.e. derived from one and the same language and therefore likely to preserve substantial likenesses, should belong to the same type.

When we come across two languages which present striking resemblances and which, for some good reason, we do not believe to be genetically related, we are inclined to assume a process of convergence determined either by protracted contacts between two communities or by some common substratum. When we have to deal with a number of languages which we suspect to have converged, it may prove useful to operate with the sort of concentrated characterization which we call a typology. If, for instance, we consider the languages spoken in the northern half of Asia, which certainly belong to different stocks, we may imagine how handy a reliable way of characterizing languages would prove for those who try to unravel the linguistic history of that part of the world through an evaluation of the duration of convergence or divergence. If this is the kind of use we have in mind when considering a linguistic typology, it is clear that phonological characteristics are likely to be just as informative and essential as any of those selected from grammar or lexicon: in a non-genetically orientated comparison of the languages of South Africa, the clicks of Zulu should play a major role.

It is, however, frequently assumed that convergence is likely to breed purely outward resemblances, the ones that result from direct imitation of some sounds, or from borrowing of lexical elements or loose grammatical items, which, since they are not welded to radicals, are easiest to isolate and to transfer from one language to another. There is some truth in this, although I am of the opinion that there is no limitation to the extent to which two languages can converge. Convergence will show in trimmings before it manifests itself in fundamentals. Therefore, if similarity is found exclusively in the structural cores of the two languages, we may be induced, when genetic relationship is ruled out, to reject as an explanation the sort of convergence that results from contacts. We may prefer to work with a theory which has division of labour and increasing social complexity as the main factors of linguistic evolution[1] so that, if by any chance their rhythm happens to be the same in two distinct communities, linguistic evolution may follow very much the same tracks in both. We might, for instance, assume that on a certain cultural and economic level we stand a good chance of coming across what has been called the ergative construction.[2] On another level, which we might consider more advanced, the ergative construction will probably have given way to an active–passive verbal opposition.

Now, if such a theory should be found to tally with at least part of the observed facts, it would entail a typology based upon such linguistic features as are likely to be most directly affected by social and economic changes: these obviously include lexical items, but also the elements that I would be tempted to call the joints, and which are the essential parts of grammar. This would certainly strengthen the traditional view according to which a non-genetic classification of languages should be based upon morpho-syntactic traits. Even if we grant that the incentives to linguistic changes are to be found among human communicative needs, still changes will not take place irrespective of the existing vocal forms, and the distinctive units of the language will prove an effec-

[1] See below, pp. 136–8.
[2] Cf. A. Martinet, 'La Construction ergative et les structures élémentaires de l'énoncé', *Journal de psychologie normale et pathologique*, 1958, pp. 377–92.

tive bulwark against random distortion.[1] But communication begins with a first analysis of experience in the frame of
the morpho-syntactic pattern of the language, and the way
this first analysis is performed seems far more fundamental
than the materials which are made use of for its transmission
to other members of the community. If carried through to its
ultimate consequences, this statement implies that not only
phonemes, but also the vocal form of meaningful units
should, in a linguistic typology, be subordinated to the
articulations of experience considered apart from the *signifiants* which are needed for their transmission: what is essential about the plural of English is not the choice of the
/z/ phoneme for its most usual rendering; it is not the fact
that /z/ alternates with /s/ and /ɪz/ in certain phonic situations; it is not either its being eked out by /ən/ in *oxen*, a
vocalic alternation in *men*, zero in *sheep* or *deer*, all this being
buttressed by verbal agreement with the subject of the clause.
These circumstances can all be lumped together as formal
accidents. No doubt, they may ultimately be instrumental
in shaping the fate of the plural category. But, from a
synchronic standpoint, they are just side issues in comparison
with the basic fact that English, unlike some other languages,
distinguishes, for certain units, between a singular and a
plural. This is an essential point to which we shall revert
below, because even the best among our predecessors have
generally missed it and concentrated on formal accidents
rather than the articulation of experience. Yet even if I
disagree with the narrowly formal approach which has been
the rule in non-genetic linguistic classifications, I do not
reject the accidents of vocal forms from linguistic typology.
Nor, for that matter, should phonological typology be dis-
sociated from one based upon other aspects of linguistic
reality. Some day, linguists may raise again the question of
whether a single spectrum can be found for characterizing
a language as a whole. But we shall have to be content with

[1] Cf. above, pp. 24–25.

separate treatments. As Charles Bazell has aptly stated, 'structural classification must start from small systems and not from languages as wholes, since the postulate of solidarity remains to be proved'.[1]

Phonological typology was one of the central preoccupations of the so-called Prague School in its early days. Among the important contributions of Trubetzkoy to the *Travaux du Cercle linguistique de Prague*, we find two classificatory surveys, one for vocalic, the other for consonantal systems.[2] It is, indeed, symptomatic of the difficulties inherent in the establishment of a linguistic typology that, even in the neatly circumscribed field of phonematics, we should have to set up two distinct systems for vowels and consonants. There may seem to exist some inverse ratio between the number of vowels and that of consonants in a given language: in a language with one or two vowel phonemes such as the ones we find in the north-western Caucasus,[3] we expect the number of consonant phonemes to exceed 50, whereas the type of French I use has barely 18 consonants to match its 16 vowels. Yet American Spanish, with 17 consonants, gets along with only 5 vocalic phonemes, and Polynesian has very short lists for both types.[4] Consequently, languages cannot be labelled either 'consonantal' or 'vocalic'. Besides, wherever we seem to discover some connexion between two patterns of consonants and vowels, it is hardly anything but numerical. It is only when consonants are found to make use of distinctive features usually restricted to vowels that we may observe some definite influence of one system on the other, since we usually notice that the vowel pattern of the language then resorts to other features: this is true, for instance, in a language like Russian in which many consonants are

---

[1] *Proceedings of the 6th International Congress of Linguists* (Paris, 1949), p. 116.
[2] *TCLP*, i (1929), pp. 39–67; iv (1931), pp. 96–116.
[3] Cf. W. S. Allen, 'Structure and System of the Abaza Verbal Complex', *TPS*, 1956, p. 129.
[4] Cf. A. Haudricourt, 'Richesse en phonèmes et richesse en locuteurs', *L'Homme*, i (1961), pp. 5–10.

opposed as fronted to non-fronted and in which, in the vocalic pattern, front is not opposed to back, but rounded to non-rounded: the /u/ phoneme is usually back ([u]), but some-times front ([y]), and the /i/ phoneme is either front ([i]), or articulated farther back ([ï]).

This type of connexion, because of its exceptional nature, only underlines the normal autonomy of the two phonematic patterns. Even if it were shown that the efforts of some linguists[1] to identify, on the plane of impressionistic acoustics, the distinctive features of vowels and consonants, do not ultimately arise from an *a priori* binaristic conception of language systems, and are supported by sufficient evidence, it would not indicate, by any means, that what is good for the vowels is either good or bad for the consonants and vice versa: should it be true, in one sense or another, that [a] is to [k] what [u] is to [p] and [i] is to [t], this would not mean that a language that presents /a/ as a phoneme should either definitely exclude /k/ from its consonantal inventory or necessarily have it.

If, on the paradigmatic plane, little is to be gained from trying to connect vocalic and consonantal systems, an attempt to characterize languages by reference to the way they balance vowels and consonants in the speech continuum may prove more successful: as is well known, some languages, Polynesian, for instance, never use a consonant without tagging a vowel after it (type *cvcv*), whereas others are not averse to consonant clusters both before and after vowels (cf. *cccvcc* in English *strict*, *cccvccc* in German *sprichst*). Some linguistic mediums (Old Church Slavic is a good example) present consonant clusters before vowels, but end all their syllables in a vowel, and they could be characterized as open-syllable languages. Modern French has a way of restricting most of its clusters to *cc* by inserting a generally non-distinctive [ə] wherever it is needed to split a larger

[1] Cf. R. Jakobson, C. Fant, and M. Halle, *Preliminaries to Speech Analysis* (Cambridge, Mass., 1952), pp. 33–34.

cluster of consonants:[1] a phrase like *je me le demande* (phone-matically /ʒmldmãd/, i.e. *cccccvc*) is, phonetically, [ʒəmləd-mãd] or [ʒmələmãd], i.e. [cvccvccvc] or [ccvccvcvc]. For typological purposes it should not prove too difficult to devise either a set of formulas of the *cvcv* type or a short repertory of labels: Georgian, with its frequent clusters of up to five successive consonants,[2] could be dubbed a heavy-cluster language, Modern French and Classical Hebrew would be 'shwa' languages, and so forth. Suchlike procedures would probably be handier and more informative than indications on a percentage basis (e.g. *c* 55 per cent.–*v* 45 per cent.). But, of course, languages are by no means always homogeneous in this matter, and many of them which, in a large majority of cases, give preference to largely vocalic syntactic patterns, may, in a few words, indulge in very heavy clusters: how many words like *extra* [/ekstra/, i.e. *vccccv*) would we have to count in French before we label it a heavy-cluster language?

This seemingly casual but probably fairly efficient classi-ficatory scheme suggests the use of an equally casual-looking procedure for dealing with the specific features of phone-matic systems. It would consist in establishing, on the basis of our present-day phonological experience, a fairly loose norm in reference to which the phonological system of a given language could be characterized by indicating in what respect it deviates from the norm, either because some of the features of that norm are missing, or because it presents phonological types that do not appear in it. Such a norm should result from a survey of a large number of the most varied languages of the world and should be set up in such a way as to achieve the tersest possible characterizations. The tentative one that follows is not meant to furnish much more than an illustration of how such a system might function.

[1] Cf. above, pp. 11–15.
[2] Cf. Hans Vogt, 'Esquisse d'une grammaire du géorgien moderne', *NTS*, ix (1938), pp. 15–16.

In order to be considered normal, the phonological pattern of a language should include two series of stops, affricates, and fricatives opposed as voiced to voiceless, lenes to fortes, or, in the case of stops and affricates, as non-aspirated to aspirated. Partaking in these two series, we should expect to find from five to ten articulatory types (orders) such as a bilabial type, a labiodental type, and so forth. It should be fairly immaterial whether stops and fricatives may or may not be conceived of as forming two parallel systems, whether, for instance, a pair like /θ/ and /ð/ should be classed as 'apicals' with /t/ and /d/, or made a separate order. Unless there were some gaps in the pattern, this should yield, as normal, ten to twenty stops (including affricates) and fricatives. English with eight pairs related as shown on the following diagram

p			t		tʃ	k
b			d		dʒ	g
	f	θ		s	ʃ	
	v	ð		z	ʒ	

or French with twelve stops and fricatives forming six orders

p	f	t	s	ʃ	k
b	v	d	z	ʒ	g

conform, in this respect, to the norm as established here.

Two to four nasal consonants, two to four 'liquids' including vibrants, laterals, and also weakly articulated spirants like English /r/ and the weak dorsal continuant called 'Parisian r', should be considered normal.

Vocalic systems with five to ten vowel phonemes would be considered average: five corresponds to the Spanish system with three degrees of aperture and two series, ten to the Danish system with four degrees of aperture and three series (if the length distinction is disregarded), in both cases with one phoneme only (/a/) for the widest degree of aperture. The existence or status of 'semi-vowels' need probably not enter into consideration here.

In reference to such a norm, the phonematics of a number of known languages could be characterized as follows:

Classical Arabic: 'emphatic' consonants, three vowels.
Finnish: a single series of consonants, gemination.
Russian: consonantal opposition between 'hard' and 'soft'.
French: nasal vowels.
English: two sets of diphthongs.
German: affricates as a distinct series.
Italian: gemination.
Castilian Spanish: stops and non-liquid continuants grouped in three series.

Such a norm, if widely accepted, would certainly render some service. But we may wonder whether we have a right to include it in a typological scheme, since it is a characterizing device pointing to deviations rather than a way of distinguishing between a limited number of types. It is, no doubt, likely that if our sampling were large enough, we would find a number of languages which deviate from the norm in just the same way: it would not be difficult to find languages that could share with Russian the consonantal opposition between 'hard' and 'soft'. But, still, the first step consisting in disregarding some differences because they are found to be very widespread, is in conflict with what is expected from a typological approach.

A real typology would probably concentrate precisely on what we disregarded when establishing our norm, namely the organization of the cores[1] of our vocalic and consonantal pattern. In this field, the pioneering efforts of N. S. Trubetzkoy must still be considered the necessary point of departure.[2]

---

[1] The notion of 'core system' is borrowed from a paper presented by Eugene Dorfman at the Chicago Meeting of the Modern Language Association on 28 Dec. 1959. It designates the occlusive-fricative section of the phonematic pattern, with whatever other consonants fit in the series and orders of that section.

[2] In *TCLP*, i (1929), pp. 39–67. Among recent attempts, cf. that of C. Voegelin in *For Roman Jakobson*, pp. 598–9, and C. Voegelin and J. Yegerlehner, 'The Scope of Whole System and Subsystem Typologies', *Word*, xii (1956),

Trubetzkoy's main distinction among vocalic systems was between triangular and quadrangular patterns: Spanish with its single open vowel was said to have a triangular pattern; Finnish, with its distinction between front /ä/ and back /a/, a quadrangular one. The French system was said to be quadrangular, but it is currently losing the distinction between front /a/ and back /ɑ/ and is therefore becoming triangular. Since the physiology of speech organs implies that there should be fewer distinctive possibilities when the jaws are wide open, triangular patterns should be considered normal and are actually more frequent. Well-balanced quadrangular patterns are rare and should be dealt with as exceptional cases rather than put on the same footing as triangular ones. The main co-ordinates of vocalic patterns are, of course, as was pointed out by Trubetzkoy, the degree of aperture and the combined play of tongue and lips determining the length and shape of the front mouth cavity. The progress of acoustic phonetic research does not imply any revision of these basic facts. Tongue-and-lip action is exceptionally of a single type, as in Adyghe, more commonly of two types (generally front-retracted versus back-rounded, hence, for maximal oral closure /i u/), as in Spanish or Italian; three types when lips and tongue act independently of each other with, as the result, /i y u/ as in French or German, or /i ɯ u/ as in Rumanian; exceptionally of four types, viz. /i y ɯ u/ as in Turkish. English, with two types of tongue-and-lip action, but with some central vowels, presents another kind of pattern. The absence of any distinction whatsoever among degrees of vocalic aperture should be quite exceptional; two degrees are well attested (in classical Arabic, for instance) though not frequent; three degrees are, probably, to be considered a norm; four degrees are not rare, but hardly very stable; since there is less space back than

pp. 444–53. Our information regarding the phonological systems of languages quoted in what follows is generally taken from N. S. Trubetzkoy's *Grundzüge der Phonologie*, Prague, 1939 (= *TCLP*, vii).

front, fewer distinctions could be expected there, which is the case in well-attested patterns such as that of seventeenth-century French;[1] more than four degrees are not likely to endure as such, neighbouring units being apt, in such patterns, to become distinct by means of some other difference than sheer aperture.

Were it not for accidents such as two distinct phonemes for the greatest aperture or a different number of relevant apertures front and back, it would be easy to devise formulae such as '23' for Spanish or Russian, '24' for Italian, '34' for Danish, where the first digit would indicate the number of distinct tongue-and-lip actions, and the second digit the number of relevant apertures. Rumanian, with /ɯ/ as head of its third tongue-and-lip type, would need some mark distinguishing its first digit, 3, from the 3 of the Danish formula, e.g. '$3_2 3$', whereas Danish would be '$3_1 3$', or '3ɯ3' vs. '3y3'.

Many languages distinguish between long and short vowels or between tense and lax ones, the passage from one type of distinction to the other being often gradual, so that both perceived duration and degree of tension contribute, for some time, to the distinction. Should we use L for duration, and T for tension, L/T for a combination of both, we could present a formula such as '33L/T' for northern German.

In some languages, like English, there is no sharp boundary between long vowels and diphthongs; the vocalic nucleus of *beat, bait, court,* and *cart* being treated as long or diphthongized depending on individual or regional usage. Here again, we could devise a formula with D_1 and D_2 for different types of diphthongs. But I doubt whether this would be worth while, since the English vocalic system is quite exceptional.

Nasal vocalic phonemes are frequent only in certain sec-

[1] Cf. A. Martinet, 'Note sur la phonologie du français vers 1700', *BSL*, xliii (1947), p. 17.

tions of the world. If their pattern is parallel to that of oral vowels, as seems to be the case in numerous African languages, we could think of such a formula as '23N' for a pattern made up of /i e a o u ĩ ẽ ã õ ũ/; archaic Parisian French, with /ɛ̃ œ̃ ã ɔ̃/, would need a separate nasal formula: 'N32'.

In many American varieties of English, one would have to take into consideration retroflex vowels, as in *park, court, hurt*, which might also require a separate formula with R as the marker. Glottalization is also to be considered a vocalic characteristic in some languages.

What is just as important as the actual number of vocalic phonemes is the extent to which the distinctions among them function: in Italian, for instance, the '24' formula given above is only true of accented vowels; elsewhere the formula is '23' as for Spanish. In some varieties of English, it could be said that all vocalic oppositions are blurred in totally unaccented syllables. But, as indicated by the last formulation, it may be preferable to deal with this type of restriction in prosodic typology.

As regards consonants, it will be useful to distinguish between the core system and a margin. The core system is made up of a number of proportions whose usual diagrammatic presentation offers a number of horizontal series, each a succession of phonemes produced at different points of the articulatory channel, but with a concomitant feature in common. What I call an order is precisely the class of phonemes articulated at the same point and with the same organs at that point; orders appear as vertical columns on the charts. For core consonants, we could devise formulas of the very same type as the ones we have been suggesting for the vowels: a first digit would indicate the number of series; a second digit the number of orders. If we leave out the nasals and, for Greek, the fricatives, the consonantal core of classical Greek would be designated as '33' (/p t k/, b d g/ /pʰ tʰ kʰ/), that of French as '26' (/p f t s ʃ k/, /b v d z ʒ g/).

Unfortunately, conflicts will arise: in English, all voiceless consonants (the ones that have a voiced partner) could be put in the voiceless series; but /tʃ/ and /ʃ/ are practically produced at the same point and with the same organs, and this is nearly true for /t/ and /θ/. Therefore they can be said to belong to the same order. This suggests that we posit two different series for voiceless phonemes, one for stops and one for fricatives, as shown on our diagram on p. 77. If we now put /t/, /d/, /θ/, and /ð/ in the same vertical row, and disregard the difference between bilabial and labiodental, we obtain, as a formula for non-nasal core phonemes, '45' instead of '28' with gaps in the stop series for the sibilants and in the fricative series for the dorsals. If, being more fastidious, we decided that /θ/ is not to /t/ what /ʃ/ is to /tʃ/ and insisted on making bilabials and labiodentals two distinct orders, our pattern would be still more lacunar.

The main objection to such formulas is the fact that they leave the prospective user in the dark regarding the nature of the distinctions between series and orders. We might, no doubt, use further indicators: e.g. for classical Greek, we might write '3VA3' where V would stand for 'voice' and A for 'aspiration', and for English '4VF5', where F would stand for 'friction'. As regards the second digit, which indicates the number of orders, it would be fairly easy to interpret it, in the case of Greek, as pointing to the three most obvious orders of labials, apicals, and dorsals, but 2 would mean 'no labials' in Iroquois, 'no apicals' in Hawaiian, 'no dorsals' in Tahitian. Besides, as was the case with vowels, gaps would be left unmarked and we would never dare multiply the second digit by the first in order to get the total number of the phonemes concerned. We could think of giving that total between parentheses, hence, for English, 4VF5(16), with 16 the real total instead of 20 suggested by 4 . . . . 5. But this would not tell us where the gaps are to be found.

We need not consider the case of the nasals and that of marginal consonants such as /l/ and /r/ in English, French, or

German, because it is quite obvious that no one would bother to learn how to decipher formulas which would have to be either incomplete and unreliable, or complete and unwieldy. Yet we need not give up all attempts. According to whether one addresses technicians or a wider linguistic public, phonematic characterizations could be secured either by the presentation of charts with series and orders, or by listing the main distinctive traits and indicating the number of phonemes affected. For classical Greek, this would give either:

b	d	g	dz		l	r		ĭ		y̆		ū
p	t	k	s					e				o
pʰ	tʰ	kʰ		h				ε̄			ɔ̄	
m	n								ă			

or, less technically (and far less accurately), 'voice and aspiration (12 ph.), 2 nasals, l, r; i-, y-, and u-types, 4 apertures, length (11 ph.)'.

None of these solutions is really satisfactory because we have found no way of combining brevity and precision. There is, in fact, among the phonemes of a language much of the same sort of solidarity as we have found among the various planes of linguistic structure: a change here will involve a change there and determine a whole chain of changes. But the existence of a given type will rarely imply the existence of another type: on being shown, for instance, the oral vocalic pattern of a language, there is no way of telling whether or not that language has nasal vowels as distinctive units. Only detailed information regarding the distribution and contextual variations of oral vowel phonemes might give a clue as to whether they have nasalized partners. A language with a /õ/ phoneme stands, of course, a good chance of having a /ẽ/ phoneme too, and a series of voiced stops seems to imply a series of voiceless ones. But this does not lead very far. Our failure to contrive a set of pregnant formulas need not affect us too much, however, since

the substantial nature of the phonemes of a language has
no direct bearing upon its actual functioning as a medium
of communication. Even the absolute or relative number
of vowels and consonant phonemes is fairly immaterial in
so far as the transmission of information is concerned: in
many cases, French, for instance, will, on the phonematic
level, be satisfactorily characterized as a *shwa*-language with
nasal vowels.

It is not a mere chance if we have, so far, found it easier
to devise terse characterizations in reference to syntagmatic
reality than for describing the relations of phonemes in the
system: coexistence in a system means distinctiveness and
consequently as much mutual independence as is compatible
with economy; coexistence in the speech continuum implies,
it is true, preservation of each successive unit's respective
identity, but also adaptation to context, i.e. a much greater
measure of solidarity. This explains why it is comparatively
easy to devise concentrated characterizations of the syntagmatic phonological features of a language, and why the field
of prosody is the one where typological research has yielded
the most satisfactory results so far.[1]

Among prosodical features, intonation is far too directly
conditioned by generally human, physiological and psychological, factors to be of any use when what it amounts to
is distinguishing among linguistic types. Only properly distinctive units, the tones, and the contrastive traits that can be
grouped under the heading of accentual prominence can be
used for typological purposes, but they do play a central role
there. In such matters, a fairly satisfactory characterization
can usually be achieved by answering, for each language, a
few questions bearing on tones and a few others concerning
accent.

1. A language has tones (distinctive tones, of course, sometimes called 'tonemes') or it has no tones: Serbo-Croatian,

---

[1] Cf. A. Martinet, *Phonology as Functional Phonetics* (London, 1949), pp. 11–
15, and 'Accent et tons', *Miscellanea Phonetica*, vol. ii (London, 1954), pp. 13–24.

Swedish, Vietnamese belong to the former type, English, Russian, Arabic to the latter.

2. A tone language may present tones on all successive intonable segments (usually syllables) or on some favoured ones only (as a rule accented ones): Southern Chinese dialects, Vietnamese, and Ibo show no speech segment without a tone; Northern (Mandarin) Chinese, Serbo-Croatian, and Lithuanian distinguish two or more tones, but only in syllables with some accentual prominence.

3. All tones may be punctual, i.e. fully characterized by their relative pitch (high, medium, or low), all of them perceptibly so, or with some easily reducible exceptions (e.g. occasional rising tones being analysed into a succession of low+high); or they may be melodic, i.e. opposed as rising to falling, as in Lithuanian, as glottalized to non-glottalized, as in Danish, as simple to complex, as in Swedish.

4. If melodic, the tones may be all on the same register as in Mandarin Chinese or in the languages just quoted; or they may be on different registers as in Vietnamese, where it is not enough to say that a tone is rising or glottalized, but where one has to state whether it is high rising or low rising, high glottalized or low glottalized.

5. Finally, the segment characterized by each tone may be the syllable, as in Serbo-Croatian, a segment smaller than the syllable, the mora, as in many languages of Central Africa, a segment larger than the syllable, such as the (polysyllabic) word in Swedish or Norwegian.

1. A language may have an accent, a prominent segment per word or comparable unit, something which is often called 'stress' in English, but accent is a functional reality, which may involve, for its actualization, stress, pitch, length, or any combination of these; or it has no accent: most European languages have an accent; Vietnamese and many Central African languages have no accent.

2. The place of the accent is either predictable and non-distinctive, or non-predictable and consequently distinctive:

it is predictable in Czech where the accent falls on the first syllable of the word, in Polish where it falls on the penult, in classical Latin where its place is determined by syllable length; it is unpredictable in Spanish where a significant unit characterized by the phoneme succession /termino/ may mean three different things according to the place of accent.

3. The distinctiveness of the place of accent is either unlimited, as in Russian, or variously limited, as in Spanish where the accent falls on one of the last three syllables of a lexical unit.

4. If in a language tones only exist under the accent, it is not unusual to say that that language has as many different accents as there are tone distinctions: thus Swedish and Lithuanian have two and Latvian three accents.

5. Most accentual languages have one accent per 'word': in Russian, *nos* 'nose' loses its accent when it combines with *rog* 'horn', in *nosorog* [nəsaˈrɔk] 'rhinoceros', which means that when two lexemes are agglutinated to serve as one, the resulting complex receives only one prominence. Other accentual languages preserve the accent of each lexeme, irrespective of whether it is free or agglutinated; but some sort of hierarchy is established among the successive accents of the same 'word': 'rhinoceros' is *Nashorn* in German, and *Nas-* (for *Nase* 'nose') and *-horn* preserve their respective prominence, with, however, a subordination of the one of *-horn* to that of *Nas-*. English shares this feature with German and extends a similar pattern to learned borrowings: *energetic* with two accents as if from **enner+getic*. It is true that English has one accent in *midland*, just like Russian in the equivalent *sredizémnyj*, and Russian has two prominent syllables in *kónuso-obráznyj* like English in the equivalent *cone-shaped*. But, although it is only statistically valid, the distinction between 'word'-accenting and lexeme-accenting languages may be retained.

The preceding sketchy survey indicates how easy it would

be to develop a system of handy labels for rapid orientation regarding the prosodical pattern of languages: German, for instance, might be said to have an initial bound-accent on the lexeme and no tone, if we exclude foreign elements; Italian accent would be described as a 'word' accent, free, but normally restricted to the last three syllables. Something could be added in both cases regarding the limitations of vocalic distinctions in unaccented syllables, and some indications concerning the make-up of both accented and unaccented syllables would not be out of place.

There would no doubt remain cases where some specific information would have to be added, if we do not want our labelling to be misleading: to say either that French has no accent or that it has a bound word-group accent would be equally unsatisfactory, because the very tenuous prominence continuing the Latin accent is one thing, the optional prominence on the initial syllable is something different, and the emphasis on and around the first consonant of the word, is different again: the true French accent is neither *impossible*, with a very slight prepausal eminence, nor *impossible*, with didactic and demarcative insistence on the initial, a very normal feature of professorial diction, nor *imp-possible* with a dramatic lengthening of [p] meant to suggest anger or passion; French has no accent in the sense English, or Russian, or Italian has, and to use one and the same label for functionally so different things would be a source of lasting confusion.

Once phonematics and prosody have been taken care of, what remains is the vast field of meaningful units and their combinations, in other words, lexicon, morphology, and syntax. Few linguists are likely to insist on establishing a lexical typology, not exactly because they feel that the lexicon of a language is too closely dependent on non-linguistic reality, but—and it may amount to the same thing—because it is what remains of the language once its neatly structured parts have been abstracted and dealt with, in other words, the domain of loosely connected units for which it would be difficult to devise a wholesale characterization.

There is, however, one criterion whose application might result in establishing interesting contrasts between languages. It is what might be called the amount of motivation[1] in the vocabulary: some languages make use of a comparatively small stock of monemes because they frequently resort to composition and derivation; their vocabulary may be said to be largely motivated: such a thing *being called* this or that because it *is* this or that. Other languages have a relatively large number of unanalysable designations; their vocabulary is thus more largely arbitrary in the Saussurian sense of the term: a thing is called thus for no discoverable reason except, perhaps, for the etymologist. The traditional illustration of this contrast is that of German, a language with a highly motivated vocabulary, and French, with a largely arbitrary one: in situations where French makes use of the two mono-monematic and highly abstract terms *monte(r)* /mõt/ and *descend(re)* /desã/ German uses combinations of two or three monemes like *aufsteigen, heraufgehen, heraufklettern,* some of these monemes being very specific and descriptive. This illustration is further supported by the remark that French speakers are generally satisfied with their thousands of loans from classical languages, most of which are unanalysable and arbitrary for the vast majority who know neither Latin nor Greek. German, on the contrary, is prone to replace foreign elements by indigenous compounds, as when *Perron* becomes *Bahnsteig, Telefon* is displaced by *Fernsprecher,* and *Automobil* by *Kraftwagen.*

It is quite probable that this contrast between motivated and arbitrary is something of which foreign linguists and local purists are more keenly aware than the average users: the present writer, a native Frenchman, had to read the diary of Ernst Jünger at the age of thirty-four before he

---

[1] Cf. F. de Saussure, *Course,* pp. 131–4, and Ch. Bally, *Linguistique générale et linguistique française,* 2nd ed. (Berne, 1944), pp. 137–9.

realized that *beaucoup de* must once have been identical with the syntagm *beau coup de*. It is by no means certain that Fr. *autostrade*, with its unidentifiable element *-strade* is more difficult to remember and to handle than its competitor *autoroute*, with its obvious ingredients. If it were shown that German children have less trouble with *Fernsprecher* than with *Telefon*, it would probably not be on account of the lack of motivation of the latter, but rather because *Fern-* and *-sprech-* sound familiar, irrespective of what they mean. The French children of today, who constantly hear the phoneme combinations /tele/ and /fɔn/ in *télévision* and *grammophone* as well as in *téléphone*, are probably just as well off as their German contemporaries even if they do not understand *télé-* and *-phone*. This, however, does not mean that motivation is to be rejected as a criterion for lexical typology, but rather that here is one more domain where one should not jump to conclusions.

In so far as the form of minimal lexical elements raises specific problems, because, for instance, they are found to vary in different surroundings, this is normally taken care of in the morphological chapter as well as in the lexical section of the description. This, after all, is as it should be, since 'morphology' is the study of form, with no specification that only the form of grammatical elements is involved. As a matter of fact, it is more or less understood that morphology deals only with the latter, and if the formal vagaries of lexemes come in into the bargain, it is because they normally result from their combination with certain grammatical items: the shift of radicals we find in *I go*, *I went*, and the formal variations we observe in *I keep*, *I kept* are taken care of in all grammars of English even if lexicographers kindly include them in their dictionaries for good measure.

Since morphology and syntax are legitimate parts of grammar, we may now state that what remains for us to investigate is grammatical typology. Traditional grammar distinguishes neatly between two main chapters: on the one hand is the study of those combinations of significant elements that may involve some formal variations or accidents (*cow, cows*, but *ox, oxen, child, children; work, worked*, but *keep, kept, sing, sang*), which normally take place within the word; this is called accidence or morphology; on the other hand, the examination of the way separate words can be combined into larger units, which is called syntax. But since there is no way of defining the term 'word' in such a way as to make the definition tally with the naïve uses of it, contemporary structuralists are prone to employ it most sparingly and to refuse to set up any universally valid linguistic unit between the moneme (often called 'morpheme') and the sentence. Formal accidents will be ascribed to monemes, not to 'words', and dealt with, for instance, as the allomorphs of a given morpheme. They will be taken care of in the course of the analysis of utterances into minimal significant units. Once the identity of these units, our monemes, is established, the linguist will have to observe how they combine. Since he has already listed and described the vagaries of moneme *signifiants*, it is by now immaterial whether the various monemes of a given context are amalgamated, agglutinated, or formally independent; the material aspect of their combination does not concern him any more. Should one insist on positing a unit intermediate between the moneme and the sentence, I would propose the syntactically autonomous or independent phrase. Such phrases would include practically all the inflected words of Latin or Greek, and also 'real' phrases such as *with the dog* and *down the road*. Still, I would not be inclined to distinguish an intraphrasal syntax, redolent of the old morphology, and an extraphrasal one which would be syntax properly so called.

Traditional non-genetic classification of languages was really based on accidence; the title of P. S. Kuznecov's short survey, *Morfologičeskaja klassifikacija jazykov*,[1] is, in fact, quite descriptive of its contents and of the way people conceived of

---

[1] In German *Die morphologische Klassifikation der Sprachen* (Halle a.d.S., 1956).

linguistic typology. If we want to formulate what it amounted to in terms of monemes, we may say that, in the last analysis, what counted was hardly anything but the degree of formal variation of individual units, for which we can set up the following scale:

1. A moneme may have the same *signifiant* throughout, whatever the combinations it enters: the relation marked, in English, by *without* is always marked by /wɪˈðaut/. This, which logically seems the most obvious solution to the problem of the formal relations of the *signifiant* with its *signifié*, has appeared, to generations of scholars blinded by their admiration for classical Indo-European languages or their ethnocentric prejudices, as a quaint and outlandish feature when applied to the expression of functions and to grammatical modifiers.

2. The *signifiant* of a moneme may vary from one context to another, but it will always be identifiable with a definite segment of the utterance: Italian *con*, 'with', normally appears as /kon/, but also as /ko/, e.g. before the masculine article (*col, coi*) and as /kol/, e.g. before the feminine article (*colla, colle*); the analysis of *colla* into *col+la* is obvious, since *la* is the normal form of the feminine article, and that of *col* into *co+l* (for **con+il*) cannot be said to be arbitrary.

3. A moneme may, in some contexts, appear as a clear-cut segment, but, in others, be merged with the *signifiant* of some other moneme (or monemes), as when Fr. *à*, which is generally /a/, even before the masculine article in *à l'hôpital* (/al . . ./), is amalgamated with that same article in *au moulin* (/o . . ./).

4. A moneme may never appear as a separate segment because its *signifiant* is always amalgamated with that of some other moneme (or monemes); still, the independent existence of the monemes involved is never endangered: in Latin, the dative moneme never appears as a segment which is not at the same time the *signifiant* of the moneme of singular or

that of plural; but Latin speakers were never at a loss to distinguish dative singular and dative plural.

5. A moneme may have a discontinuous *signifiant*, its use by the speaker implying some formal modifications in two or more different places in the utterance: the Latin moneme usually identified as *sine*, 'without', was necessarily accompanied by a specific ('ablative') ending of the nouns whose function was being indicated, so that, in *sine dubio*, its *signifiant* included /sine/, plus the /. . . ō/ of *dubio*, in which, however, the *signifiant* of the singular moneme was amalgamated. The plural moneme of French may show as a single segment, e.g. as /. . . e . . ./ in *dans les champs* /dãleʃã/ (cf. the singular *dans le champ* /dãlʃã/); but it may also appear in the form of several successive accidents, e.g. as /. . . e . . . z . . . o . . . m/ in *les petits animaux dorment* /leptizanimodorm/ as opposed to *le petit animal dort* /lptitanimaldor/.

There is, however, another feature which has to be considered if we want to account for the pronouncements of former typologists: that is the degree to which two monemes, appearing in immediate succession and in a definite relationship, may be separated by the insertion of some new element. As a matter of fact, inseparability is one of the most useful criteria for distinguishing what is formally one word from what is a succession of different words.[1] In any case, it is the one that generations of scribes and writers have adopted, as a rule, throughout the centuries of alphabetic writing practice, when they have endeavoured to divide the written continuum of each language into those segments which constitute our graphic 'words'; German spellings like *aufgeben*, *aufgebe*, each written as one block in spite of the possibility of inserting something between *auf* and the rest (*aufzugeben*, *ich gebe es auf*), represent shocking exceptions for whoever is not awed by the majesty of spelling traditions. In view of the paramount role played by the notion of 'word' in former typological speculations, it is fair to single out all the aspects

---

[1] Cf. *Proceedings of the 6th Intern. Congress, Paris*, 1949, pp. 293-4.

of linguistic reality that afford some justification for the use of such an ill-defined concept. Yet a clear-cut distinction between inseparability, total or partial, and variation of *signifiants* is fully justified only on a strictly synchronic plane. It is indeed clear that inseparability is conducive to formal accidents which ultimately result in amalgamation: phonetic evolution will tend to merge successive elements in the utterance, and this can be counteracted only inasmuch as the elements in question may, at any time, cease to be in contact; any limitation of the latitude to combine monemes freely is the first step toward eventual coalescence, semantic as well as formal. When what is at stake is a general characterization of languages, from a synchronic angle, no doubt, but on a wide temporal scope, widespread inseparability will be found to have bred some degree of formal overlapping and amalgamation, so that the two features normally go together.

Sapir's outstanding merit was to discover and point out that the traditional approach to non-genetic classification was founded upon a fairly casual rating of the frequency and degree of formal adhesion, overlapping, and coalescence. He therefore recommended a typology that would not be based exclusively upon features which might not be so fundamental as many scholars had believed them to be. As a matter of fact, observation had revealed that most languages presented a mixture of various formal types, and comparative evidence had indicated that formal features were subject, through time, to considerable variations either towards syntagmatic coalescence or away from it. Without rejecting what he called degrees of 'fusion' and the traditional 'synthetic' $\sim$ 'analytic' opposition, Sapir concentrated on 'the nature of the concepts expressed by the language' and made it the real foundation of his classificatory attempt. He thereby undoubtedly went farther and deeper than any of his predecessors. A proof of this is that, to this day, forty years after the publication of Sapir's book, anyone who deals with language classification necessarily uses Sapir's analysis either as a starting-point or as a frame of reference. Yet, for all its perspicuity, it stands as a nearly tragic illustration of the pitfalls of psychologism.

Sapir's original contribution centres around a conceptual analysis of language elements starting from the acceptable view that we should find, in all languages, significant units that do not carry in themselves a mark of their relation to the rest of the utterance, say, *chair, lamp,* and others, such as *with* or *for,* that are expressly meant to indicate what sort of relations the former keep with each other. This leaves out the theoretical possibility of a language entirely made up of words of the *yesterday* type, which stand, at the same time, for some element of experience: 'the day before this day', and the relation of that element to the rest of the experience: 'as the segment of time when . . .'. But we know that economy rules out any such language, and we may agree with Sapir that all known languages utilize monemes with the *chair* type of function, and monemes having the *with* type of function. Our criterion for distinguishing between one type and the other is not semantic, however, but positional: if *chair* by itself is to have a function in an utterance, it must stand in a well-determined position in relation to the other elements of the utterance; but this changes as soon as a moneme of the *with* type is added to it: the phrase *with (the) chair* will not depend on its relative position for the expression of its function. The importance of this reliance on formal criteria will appear in what follows.

As a third type of element, Sapir poses what he calls 'derivational concepts', which formally correspond to affixes. There can be little objection to this, except that, of course, his conceptual approach prevents him from connecting composition and derivation, which are such closely related phenomena that the analyst is often at a loss to say, in concrete cases, whether a given moneme is an affix or an element of a compound word: in contemporary French, some speakers use the form *bus* as an abbreviation of *autobus*; this form was probably used first in imitation of its English equivalent, and it is not in general use yet; for those who use it, *autobus* is a compound word of the *autoroute* 'motor-road' type; for those who do not, it is a derivative of the *electrobus* type, with *bus* as a suffix. The formal criterion of both derivation and composition is, of course, a combinatory comportment of derivatives and compounds which is, in all respects, identical with that of corresponding single monemes. It is, no doubt, quite essential to determine whether a language makes use of derivation, or composition, or both: languages vary a good deal in that respect. But this has little to do with the distinction between monemes that do not indicate their relations to the context (dependents) and those that are meant to mark those relations (functionals); both composition and derivation yield units which may function as dependents (*farm-yard*, *yellowish*) or as functionals (*on-to*, Lat. *in-ter*, *in-tr-ā*, *in-tr-ō*). We have here a distinct type of linguistic activity, which we could dub lexical, or, more generally, paradigmatic expansion. Any typology will have to take this into account in connexion with the lexicon, a domain in which, as we have seen, the frequency of still analysable compounds and derivatives could be characterized in terms of motivation.

Sapir further distinguishes between 'pure relational concepts' of the *with* type, and 'concrete relational concepts', but he never makes perfectly clear where the difference between the two types actually lies. It would seem that this distinction more or less parallels that between what we call functionals and modifiers, the grammatical elements which secure autonomy, and those which do not. But his conceptual approach misled him into expressing the difference in terms of degree of abstraction, and made him fall a victim to the common illusion that some grammatical words or items (his 'pure relational concepts') have no meaning. If meaning is to be mentioned in linguistics at all, it should be defined as resulting from the necessity, for the speaker, of choosing at a point among several units for the expression of some element of experience. Choice, on that level, implies meaning, and meaning is there only if there has been a choice. Syntactic functions, such as the ones expressed by prepositions or cases, are, in a way, predetermined: a dative relation is expected after a verb meaning 'to give'. But the choice often exists between the presence of the dative complement and its absence: *advice* can be *given* absolutely or specifically *to someone*. A grammatical subject, as such, is an item whose presence does not result from a choice: the speaker does not choose to use a subject or not, because, by definition, as it were, a subject is what *must* be added to a predicate to make a statement in those languages where we have a right to speak of a subject. Therefore, since the introduction of the subject function is never a matter of choice, we may say it is deprived of meaning. A formal consequence of this is a tendency to eliminate any mark of the subject function, so that a zero *signifiant* should correspond to a zero *signifié*. But this is an extreme case. The difference between functionals and modifiers, i.e. the two types of grammatical monemes, should not be expressed in semantic terms, although modifiers are likely to be semantically richer than functionals. It should be based upon the part each type plays in the sentence. The notion of relation, which Sapir used in order to give a semblance of unity to his non-lexical units, is extremely vague and misleading: there is no doubt that a definite article normally involves some relation to what precedes, since one of its normal functions is to indicate that the accompanying being, object, or notion has been previously mentioned. But this role is in no way distinct from that of pointing to the fact that the being, object, or notion is universally known, as when we say *the sun*, *the King*, or *the lion* for the species. The definite article is not indicative of any relationship; it is the mark of some specific information added to the communication, just like any other modifier such as 'singular' or 'plural'. It summarizes some previous information, but gives no indication as to what the function of its environment is in the linguistic rendering of the experience which is being communicated. Amalgams may make it difficult, in many cases, to decide which phonic segment is to be ascribed to a functional, and which to a modifier. But, functionally, the two types are fundamentally different. The distinction is not, as Sapir has it, between material content and relation, but between functional monemes and non-functional ones, the latter including the bulk of what Sapir puts under 'material content', namely lexicon, including elements of composition and derivation, together with our modifiers.

It is, as we have seen, by no means impossible to find functional justifications for every one of Sapir's four conceptual groups. But this does not mean that we can retain Sapir's analysis as the foundation of a typology that transcends formal accidents. Once we have ruled out reference to things meant as a principle of linguistic classification, it becomes clear that the four types of facts are not comparable and that it makes no sense to consider them along a scale leading from pure conceptual to pure relational. Should we try to classify monemes according to their function, we should first put on a plane of its own the distinction between derivational monemes and the rest. The latter could not very well be dubbed non-derivational, since the fact of being derivational implies nothing but a limitation, in the distribution, to cases of paradigmatic expansion, in other words, a negative feature. We certainly would not want to have to specify 'non-derivational' every time we characterize a moneme affected by no such limitation. Once the problem of derivationals is set aside, our two criteria would be functional indication and grammaticality. By combining them, we would obtain four types again, as shown on the diagram on p. 98, out of which only three (viz. 1, 3, and 4) could be found parallel to those of Sapir.

1	2
lexical without indication of function *chair* type	grammatical without indication of function *the* type
3 lexical function indicating *yesterday* type	4 grammatical function indicating *with* type

Two of them (1 and 2) would not partake in functional
indication or, in other words, would not confer, to themselves
or others, what we have called syntactic autonomy: the
ones (1) would be lexical dependents, the others (2) either
grammatical dependents such as pronouns, or grammatical
determinants, i.e. modifiers. The remaining two would be
autonomous monemes of the *yesterday* type (3) and autonomy
conferring grammatical items, i.e. functionals (4). Predicatives, as such, would not all belong to the same one of the two
lexical types, since they might be said to be dependent where
they can be orientated (in languages with both active and
passive voices), but autonomous, even independent elsewhere.

Furthermore, there is a fundamental difference between
Sapir's groups and our types, which makes it impossible for
us to utilize the precedent. When we say that our types are
functional, we imply that a given item may belong to different types: in a large number of languages, the same
moneme is used predicatively as the equivalent of 'to give'
and as a functional with the value of 'dative'; this, of course,
does not entail that all predicatives can be used as functionals or all functionals as predicatives. In Basque, the
moneme *-ko* is used either as a functional (*etxe-ko* 'of the
house') or as a derivational use for lexical expansion (*etxeko-
a-k* 'the domestics'; *-a-k* = 'the'+plural); here again, this
does not mean that all functionals of Basque can be used as
derivationals, but it indicates that our types are not mutually
exclusive. We should not operate as if a given language *had*
or *had not* modifiers or functionals, but assume that any

language is likely to have monemes *acting* as functionals. Therefore we cannot follow Sapir when he classifies languages according to whether they 'express concepts' of this or that group of his, which, in less-guarded parlance, would have been expressed as 'having' this or that sort of units: beside his group I (of 'basic concepts'), which he sensibly assumes to be universal, a given language should use, for the expression of relations, either his group IV (of 'pure relational concepts') or his group III (of 'concrete relational concepts'); of his four, A, B, C, D, classes, two (A and B) combine I and IV, and two (C and D) combine I and III; the absence of derivation distinguishes A from B and C from D. Groups IV and III are thus presented as mutually exclusive, which rules out any attempt to preserve some parallelism between our types and Sapir's groups: when Sapir conceived of his group III, he must have had in mind concepts corresponding to our modifiers; when he set up his group IV, he certainly wanted to include in it elements corresponding to prepositions, which are the most obvious of our functionals, and position, as a mark of function, is expressely mentioned in this connexion; but the lack of perspicuity inherent in the conceptual approach led him to list English and French among languages that make no use of his group IV, thereby disregarding the fact that in both languages the relations of nominals with the rest of the utterance are, in the overwhelming majority of cases, indicated by means of position or prepositions. It would be interesting to look for the features of these two languages, such as widespread amalgamation, concord, and discontinuous monemes of all sorts, that must have been instrumental in obscuring for him such an obvious fact. But this would lead us too far. It will suffice to point out here that, even in his conceptual classification, Sapir is so dependent on form and intent upon finding formal differences supporting his conceptual grouping, that he indicates, as the only normal expression of his 'concrete relational concepts' (group III), affixation and inner modification, the use of independent word being reserved to that of 'pure relational concepts' (group IV).

As soon as each utterance in any language is conceived of as a succession of minimal signs, with or without over-lappings, it becomes clear that grammar can be presented as the set of rules restricting the free combinations of all these signs. A grammatical typology is bound to start from the various types of restrictions that have been, inductively or deductively, identified. We have seen, in a preceding chapter,[1] that a language can hardly be conceived of without such restrictions, for instance, regarding the extent to which the various monemes may assume the various existing functions. Some monemes must necessarily be identified as endowed with functions and others as functional indicators. This accounts for the fact that there is no language recorded in which one should not somehow distinguish between gram-matical and lexical items, whether these be opposed as empty words to full words, or as grammatical categories to basic concrete units. Restrictions on the free use of the different lexemes in all the existing functions are probably to be found everywhere, but in many cases these may result from the specific meaning of some lexemes: a thing may not be used as an agent; some predicates cannot be passively orientated. But what may be peculiar to some languages and therefore typologically relevant are wholesale restrictions resulting in splitting the lexical repertory into neatly contrasting classes.

In this respect the most fundamental dichotomy is the one between languages in which all lexical monemes can be found performing the same basic functions, and those, prob-ably a clear majority in the world of today, in which some monemes, which we may designate as 'verbal', are specialized and restricted to predicative uses: on the one hand, we have languages in which the equivalent of 'tree' and 'it stands upright', of 'leg' and 'it walks' are identical and distin-guished only by the predicative use of the latter, some non-

[1] Cf. above, pp. 63–64.

predicative function for the former; on the other hand, forms of speech in which the equivalents of 'tree' or 'leg' may perhaps be found to act as predicates, whereas those of 'it stands' and 'it walks' can be predicate and nothing else.

Languages with a special 'verbal' class restricted to predicative use can be further subdivided into languages in which non-verbal lexemes can normally be used with predicative function and those in which this is formally impossible. Russian is a language in which lexemes endowed with 'nominal' functions are also found as predicates. On the contrary, English is a language in which 'verbal' monemes have a practical monopoly of predicative function, and it illustrates a linguistic type where a given lexical item is always used either predicatively (verb) or non-predicatively (noun or adjective); in regular, out-of-situation, syntax, no statement is possible without some verbal form.

Another fundamental distinction should be made between languages in which the predicative moneme, once it has been selected, can only stand in one definite relation to every one of the other elements of the utterance, and languages in which the predicative moneme can be orientated in different ways in order to give prominence to its relationship with one of the other elements. This means, in traditional parlance, that great importance should be attached to whether a language distinguishes or not, in what we may call its conjugation, between an active voice and one or more so-called passive voices. This feature may be connected with the presence of a subject properly so called, i.e. the compulsory use of an item accompanying the predicate and whose relation to it is accordingly established as preferential and fundamental.

All this amounts to saying that the foundations of a linguistic typology are to be looked for in the way in which each language community proceeds to analyse experience into a number of elements in such a way that the linear order of their succession will not prevent hearers from perceiving the nature of their mutual relations and thus reconstructing the total experience. The basic syntactic patterning of each language has to be presented in terms of minimal significant units, the monemes, each moneme being conceived as the habit of identifying some definite facet of experience with some formal distinction. There are thus always two faces to every moneme. It would be linguistically ideal to have a situation where the formal face of every moneme would be always the same and correspond to a neatly analysable segment. In fact, the *signifiant* of a given moneme may vary according to context, be discontinuous, or merge with neighbours, so that only functional identity salvages the unity of the moneme. A fundamentally synchronic description of a language should go beyond these formal accidents, and reach the essentials: the resources of a language as an instrument of communication.

IV

LINGUISTIC VARIETY

IN this world of ours where, apart from pitiful exiles, every man is supposed to owe allegiance to some ruler or State, this allegiance is tacitly assumed to imply the use of one and the same language: an Englishman speaks English and a Frenchman speaks French. Belgians are widely believed to speak 'Belgian', a belief that is partially substantiated by the existence of Flemish. It took two world wars to convince the French that the British and the Americans were different nations, but the realization of their separateness carried along with it the by now well-entrenched belief in the existence of a fully distinct American language. We all, in daily life, speak, and sometimes act, as if there existed neatly circumscribed language communities wherein all members are expected to behave linguistically in exactly the same way. Those who do not, in all details, are said to speak with an 'accent' if their deviations from an assumed norm are mainly phonic. They are supposed to speak a 'dialect' if their aberrance extends to grammar and lexicon, particularly if communication is thereby somewhat impaired.

As long as linguists were 'philologists' who mainly concentrated on written, literary forms of human communication, they were not inclined to take exception to this sketchy and naïve approach to socio-linguistics: 'accents' were hardly ever noticeable as such in their texts, and 'dialects' were best forgotten about except, perhaps, in the isolated case of ancient Greek.

But even after they have become conscious of the basically vocal form of language, after decades of efforts devoted by many of them to the collection of dialectal material, they still seem to take it for granted that there are well-identified objects called 'language communities' whose members speak alike in all respects. At least most of them behave and write as if they did. In this matter there is little difference between 'traditionalists' and 'structuralists': all would seem to believe in the perfect unity of each language. Among the latter, few would hesitate to posit that French has so many (e.g. 34) phonemes, or that the /s/ of Spanish is apico-alveolar, even if they were ready to grant, when challenged, that many French speakers use less, and many others more, than thirty-four phonemes, and that millions of Spanish speakers, in Spain and elsewhere, use dorso-alveolar sibilants.

The homogeneity of linguistic communities is a useful pragmatic assumption, at least at a certain stage of linguistic research. If languages are, first and foremost, instruments of communication, it is fairly natural that we should assume, at least as an ideal, that all people who use one of them share the bundles of articulatory habits and vocal reactions to various stimuli whose sum total we call a language: communication would be best secured if all people concerned spoke exactly in the same way. Some variety is no doubt welcome in human affairs. But when efficiency is at stake, relevancy is what counts exclusively. But unbiased observation shows that when people understand each other they do so in spite of differences which affect not only irrelevant trimmings, but sometimes fundamentals. It is true that when we look at things from a dynamic angle, the prospect clears up a little: it is comforting to notice that when people actually communicate they tend to identify their speech habits and linguistic reactions: communicating improves communication and does it apace. But this might eventually result in the complete unification of linguistic communities only if it worked within their confines exclusively, which is by no means the case. Linguistic convergence is universal: just like charity, it begins at home and, just like charity, it extends to the whole of mankind; it takes place among those who feel they belong to the same language and social group and believe they speak alike in all respects, as between a new-comer and the former residents in a suburban district; but it takes place just as well among Russian and Norwegian fishermen who happen to settle in the same neighbourhood along the Arctic shore, and results in the development of a new form of speech.[1] Besides, convergence will inevitably breed divergence: the new-comer who adapts his speech to that prevailing in his new surroundings will thereby deviate from what had been his set of linguistic habits so far, and all the quicker if the original linguistic differences between the two parties did not hamper immediate oral communication. As long as communicative needs differ from one district to another, complete linguistic homogeneity cannot exist.

If it has taken so long for such an obvious fact to be acknow-ledged, it is again because those who were interested in matters of language concentrated on literary forms of com-munication. Those forms had early assumed a large measure of unification since they were used by somewhat restricted groups of literate people engaged in a sort of communication which did not require the establishment of physical contact and which, consequently, could easily spread to the most distant provinces.

Once the familiar and comfortable idea of the homo-geneity of linguistic communities is abandoned, the world appears as an ocean of conflicting attractions, convergence here breeding divergence there, with new centres of attrac-tion developing at all times and threatening to disrupt existing ensembles. And this is true on all levels, national, provincial, local, and familial. In the practice of descrip-tive linguists the growing realization of this endless linguistic variety has led to the position that if a linguistic description has to be consistent, it must be that of an idiolect, i.e. the language as spoken by a single individual. But does this not contradict our assumption that language is above all an

---

[1] See Olaf Broch, 'Russenorsk', *Archiv für slavische Philologie*, xli (1927), pp. 209–62.

instrument of communication? Besides, if we want to do justice to all the implications of the ceaseless turmoil we have just sketched, we cannot be satisfied with limiting our observation to one single individual, since that individual will not handle his language tomorrow in exactly the same way as he does today or did the day before. The idiolect, as a frame of linguistic description, needs to be precisely dated.

At this stage, and before we proceed, it may be useful to stress that the rather startling picture that has just been presented is no fiction, but that it is derived from factual observation: when, in 1941, sixty-six French officers, born and reared in Paris, were asked some forty-odd simple questions, such as 'Do you pronounce *patte* and *pâte* alike?', which were meant to reveal the main features of their respective vocalic system, no two of them agreed in all respects, although their phonological comportment as a whole contrasted with that of their 343 non-Parisian comrades who also answered the questionnaire.[1]

As regards the evolution an idiolect may undergo through time, the present writer may be allowed to refer to a sketch of the system of French vowels he published in 1933.[2] In that first attempt to present a phonological analysis of that language, being still unaware of the existing latitude in such matters, he identified his then system with that of French at large, and posited two long phonemes /y:/ and /œ:/ as distinct from /y/ and /œ/ on account of such minimal pairs as *sûr–sure* (/syr/~/sy:r/), *seul–seule* (/sœl/~/sœ:l/). When reconsidering his phonological practice, some years later, he noticed that these distinctions of length had been wiped out, probably under the influence of his Parisian surroundings.

If such variations from speaker to speaker and, with the same speaker, from one period to another, are attested in the realm of phonology, a domain where people as a rule are

---

[1] Cf. *Prononciation* generally, and *Phonology as Functional Phonetics*, pp. 36–37.
[2] 'Remarques sur le système phonologique du français', *BSL*, xxxiv (1933), pp. 191–202.

least conscious of what they do, they can hardly be doubted in the fields of syntax and lexicon. The practical conclusion to be derived from this is that a linguistic description that is not expressly that of a dated idiolect should be expected to subsume divergent usages. If existing variations are not sacrificed on the altar of descriptive simplicity and are duly presented, the result will be the establishment of some sort of hierarchy among linguistic oppositions: some distinctions are found to be universal among the members of the group under consideration; others are found to be kept by some members only and to be disregarded by other members. If the language at stake is American English as a whole, it will be pointed out that *horse* and *hoarse*, *morning* and *mourning* are kept distinct by some speakers, while others pronounce them alike, and this type of distinction will not be put on the same level as that between *card* and *cord*, *lard* and *lord* which seems to be universal. In describing French in general, it cannot be said that *près* differs from *prés* in the same way as *pris* differs from *prés*, although physically the three vowels are close to cardinal [i e ɛ], because *all* French speakers distinguish *prés* from *pris*, but millions identify *prés* and *près*.

We can conclude from all this that the notion of linguistic community is not only useful, but unavoidable in linguistics as soon as a language is conceived as an instrument of communication constantly adapting itself to the needs of the group who make use of it; 'communication' implies 'community'. But in order not to let this term confuse linguistic issues, it is indispensable to stress a number of well-established facts.

1. No community is linguistically homogeneous: no two persons use a language in exactly the same way; the same situation will elicit different linguistic reactions from different onlookers; no two persons will use or understand the very same vocabulary; even the highly structured aspects of language, such as phonology and morphology, may differ in important matters from one speaker to another without

impairing mutual understanding and even without being
noticed by the interlocutors.

2. Many people belong to two, or more than two, communities. This is, of course, the case in such well-known
bilingual stretches as Brussels, Alsace, or South Africa. But
this applies to many situations where both a vernacular and
a standard language are alternately used by the same people
with different interlocutors. From a linguistic standpoint
we cannot make bilingualism depend on the amount of
prestige enjoyed by the two forms of speech in contact. The
alternate use of two different phonological systems is probably
the least ambiguous test of a bilingual situation.

3. Many people use concurrently different styles of the
same language. The same Frenchman may use from one
minute to the next two totally different equivalents of 'shall
we go?'; the literate *partons-nous?* or the slangy *on les met?*
with the familiar plural first person pronoun *on*.

4. Many people who do not use more than one style or one
language understand different styles or different languages.
Passive knowledge of languages and unimpeded aural understanding of various not actively used styles is of frequent
occurrence and should play a great role in the correct appreciation of socio-linguistic situations.

Before we examine in detail cases where people cannot help
being aware of linguistic differences, it is important to revert
to definitely unilingual situations where the different members of the community are not aware of any such deviation
in the speech of others or in their own as could be dubbed
'accent' or 'dialect'. In these the communicative ideal of
language seems fully realized: it really does not matter in the
least whether the speech of one man is physically identical
with that of another provided possible divergences do not
interfere with the free and easy transmission of experience. In
this respect it is quite essential that all participants should be
intimately convinced that they speak 'the same language': since
language is constantly redundant, words having generally

more phonemes than is strictly necessary to keep them distinct from others in given contexts, and messages being as a rule more profuse than logic would demand, a few divergences will not prevent nor even impair mutual understanding. People being normally intent upon understanding what is said, and hardly upon observing the way it is said, they will never notice any such divergence. Language works best when it is not noticed as such, and speakers will be better off as long as they manage to forget about it. This is why they are apt to get impatient and scornful when some 'accent' or 'dialect' feature reminds them that linguistic communication can be a problem. Unexpected deviations may prove misleading even if they do not affect the distinctive and significant pattern: if I have never heard my /a/ phoneme pronounced as anything but [a], an occasional [ɑ] rendering may be startling and may keep me wondering for a split second whether that unexpected sound 'meant' something, even if the nearest vowel in the system is some distant /ɔ/ phoneme. But if one is used to hearing something that deviates from one's own practice, that something will certainly pass unnoticed: if I pronounce my /a/ phoneme as [a] but am quite used to hearing [ɑ] for the same unit, no [ɑ] pronunciation can ever ruffle me except, perhaps, if it comes from someone from whom I do not expect anything but [a].

In this connexion I may perhaps be allowed to present an illustration borrowed from my own experience: as a child I knew that my mother's French was slightly tainted by her early use of a Franco-Provençal dialect and that, on the other hand, when she spoke that dialect there was something that did not sound quite right. One day, about the age of twenty, I was sitting in an orchard reading for an examination. My mother was conversing with her sister, about ten yards away. At some point she happened to mention the name of the famous political leader Marat and pronounced it [maʁa] with a dorsal spirant. This startled me out of my reading and, half jokingly, I told my mother she had no right to pronounce that name otherwise than [mara], i.e. with a trill. It suddenly had dawned upon me that she used both 'rolled' and 'non-rolled' *r*, which explained why her French sounded provincial and her dialect Frenchified, but that she usually had the trill for single intervocalic *r* of the spelling and the dorsal spirant for -*rr*-. Her use of the latter in *Marat*, probably as an imitation of the teacher from whom she had first heard the name, had suddenly made me realize that I expected from her a tongue tip [r] wherever the spelling had a single *r*.

Generally speaking everything one has grown up with belongs to one's universe, and this applies to linguistic experience as well as to any other domain. Anything we have heard in the course of the acquisition of our language is felt to be part of that language. This does not, by any means, imply that we ourselves shall make use of everything we readily accept from others: a number of words, certain pronunciations, we have heard from people we either do not approve of or dare not imitate, and these we avoid. But this remains unconscious until, by chance, we are startled by hearing them in an unexpected situation or context.

Something similar applies to different generations in each other's company: we hear in the speech of older people many turns and traits which we would never use, but which still belong to our language. Yet our grandchildren will never get used to them and these features will thus gradually disappear, first only from active use as long as we live, then also as acceptable forms as soon as only those generations remain on earth that have never heard them. What we have heard ever since we could perceive what was said around us is always part of our language as we conceive it, even if we may exceptionally become aware of the obsolescence of certain terms or elements.

Linguistic variety on a large scale, within one and the same community, is, by both laymen and linguists, usually dealt with in terms of dialects. Other terms such as patois, brogue, *bable*, *Platt*, refer to varieties which are ultimately presented under the rubric of dialectology. Any attempt on the part of specialists to use these terms without previous redefinition is likely to be unsatisfactory because they are, in fact, quite unspecific designations used, with a touch of contempt, by standard speakers in reference to any speech variety that is not socially acceptable. The *American College Dictionary* defines *patois* as 'any peasant or provincial form of speech', which amounts to authorizing the use of that term for any language variety except some metropolitan standard. Such a definition, which reflects social prejudices rather than the realization of real linguistic differences, makes the word useless for our purposes unless we decide to define it in our own terms.

When we try to approach this problem from a linguistic angle, it is disappointing to find that little can be done if we start from those achievements of which we are so proud, viz. our phonological and morphological patterns. Here is my wife's vocalic pattern in French in absolute final position presented side by side with mine:

i	y	u		i	y		u
e	ø	o		e	ø		o
	a			ε		ə	
				a		ɑ	

These look very different. But it happens that contacts between people with such divergent vocalic systems have been so frequent during, say, the last two centuries, that the French language is handled in such a way to render the confusion of /a/ and /ɑ/, /e/ and /ε/, /ø/ and /ə/ (as in *sur ce* = *sur ceux*) perfectly innocuous. Only someone intent upon detecting phonological differences would think of my wife's speech and my own as two distinct varieties. The only valid criterion in such matters is less perhaps the ease of understanding, which we would not know how to measure, than the existence of bilingualism, in the widest sense of the word,

namely, the use by the same persons of two different phonological and morphological patterns depending on one's interlocutors. We would thus need a term, say, 'dialect$_1$', to refer
to linguistic forms used by unilinguals in their oral communications with any other member of the community, even
those who use some other dialect$_1$: the New York City form
of speech and the Chicago form of speech would thus be
labelled two dialects$_1$ of American English, since a speaker of
one would not hesitate to use his own form of speech when
addressing a speaker of the other. Another term, say 'dialect$_2$',
would designate linguistic forms used as a vernacular by
bilinguals in their communications with some particular
members of the community, whereas they use a dialect$_1$ with
the other members; the speakers of any dialect$_2$ are, in fact,
a smaller (provincial) community within the larger (national)
community. This type of situation will be amply illustrated in
what follows.

It is clear that dialects$_2$ are likely to be more divergent than
dialects$_1$, since if they were not and if, accordingly, their use
did not hamper mutual understanding, speakers of dialects$_2$
would not take the trouble of learning a dialect$_1$ which is not
their vernacular. But this greater divergence is not included
in the definition because it is, as we have seen, too difficult to
measure.

Whether dialects$_1$ all enjoy the same prestige, or whether
one of them, or a group of them, ranks higher and is, therefore, no longer considered a dialect, but the standard, is
again a different matter: prestige is difficult to measure and
had better not intervene in linguistic classifications. Still, it is
important to be aware of such extremes as the situation in the
United States, where no regional standard can be localized,
and that in Italy, where the Tuscan varieties, when deprived of their strictly local features, rank definitely higher
than other dialects$_1$, which are, of course, and in contradistinction to dialects$_2$, local forms of the national language.
It is worth remembering that the original use of 'dialect' in

ancient Greece, before the establishment of Athens' cultural hegemony, corresponds to our 'dialect$_1$' and reflects a linguistic situation far more similar to the American than to the Italian one.

It could be objected that if dialect$_2$ necessarily implies bilingualism in contradistinction to dialect$_1$, it would be better and clearer to call dialect$_2$ a language, a term which is implied in 'bilingual'. But a language is understood to enjoy a status which can by no means be granted to many dialects$_2$ that only survive as the impoverished mediums of retarded rural segments of a community. The widespread reluctance to speak of bilingualism in the case of situations involving dialects$_2$ is due precisely to the impression that they are granted thereby a status they do not deserve.

The dialectal situation in France has long been the subject of careful and detailed studies, and although professional dialectologists have widely disregarded some of the distinctions which we today find basic, these studies have largely contributed to making France one of the best fields if we want to illustrate linguistic variety within one and the same community.

It cannot be said that France, as a political entity, coincides with a linguistic community, since millions of unilingual French speakers live in other countries such as Belgium, Switzerland, and Canada. But it cannot be doubted that anywhere in France people are supposed to be able to handle their public and private affairs in French: all children living in France are expected to attend schools where French is taught as a subject and at the same time is the medium through which other subjects are taught; furthermore, all able-bodied males spend an average of two years in an army in which French is the only official medium. As a result of this, non-French-speaking Frenchmen must be rare except among older people, chiefly women and mainly in Alsace and the traditionally Frankish-speaking fringe of Lorraine.

At the present day a definite majority of the 45 million residents of France must be unilingual French speakers, which, of course, does not mean that they all speak alike. All of them could be said to make use of dialects$_1$, i.e. different varieties of French, but this would by no means reflect the way the French react to such variations: deviations from what is felt to be the norm in matters of pronunciation are labelled 'accents'; other aberrances, if startling, might be considered 'patois' by those who would be tempted to apply this term to any departure from the norm. The few competent people who have dealt with French dialects$_1$ refer to them as *français locaux*. Some of them have been summarily described.[1] They are certainly well attested in Gilliéron's *Atlas*,[2] but there is no way of knowing with certainty whether what we find at a certain point is dialect$_1$ or dialect$_2$. In a radius of sixty miles around Paris, Gilliéron's forms are likely to originate from unilinguals and therefore to represent local French (dialects$_1$). In the southern half of the country all notations, with very few exceptions, should represent utterances from bilinguals who knew French at least well enough to understand Edmont's questions and who *translated* the French words into the local dialect$_2$. But, in between, the forms attested in many places are of such a nature as to authorize any one of the two interpretations.

Unilingual France is expanding rapidly. The First World War was fatal to dialects$_2$ in many sections of the country: all fit men between the ages of eighteen and fifty went to war. At first they were in locally mustered regiments, but very soon, heavy losses resulted in successive amalgamations, as a result of which soldiers from all parts of the country could be found in the same unit. This meant that there was little use for dialects$_2$ at the Front and behind it, except when such a

---

[1] e.g. *Le Français parlé à Toulouse*, by Jean Séguy (Toulouse, 1950) (*Bibliothèque Méridionale* publiée sous les auspices de la Faculté des lettres de Toulouse, 1st series, XXVIII), 132 pp.

[2] About the *Atlas linguistique de la France* by J. Gilliéron and E. Edmont, see Sever Pop, *La Dialectologie*, I. *Dialectologie romane* (Louvain, n.d.), pp. 113–36.

one was still practised and understood over a large area so that there might remain, in some regiments, groups of soldiers who found it easier to use it among themselves than French. On returning home, those who for close on four years had been using French almost exclusively insisted on speaking French to their children, and their wives eventually followed suit. This explains why, in large sections of present-day rural France, dialects$_2$ are frequently understood but hardly spoken by people under forty. It is likely that the Second World War has sealed the fate of a good many of those which had fully survived the First. The very possibility of a dialect disappearing through a break in the transmission is a clear indication that that dialect is a dialect$_2$. A dialect$_1$ cannot disappear, since, in the case of unilinguals, it is the only form of speech at their disposal. The effect of a war will be to make it closer, if not to the 'standard', at least to the average form of speech.

It is a great pity that Gilliéron was not aware of the necessity of distinguishing between the two types of dialect and consequently did not try to devise a way of drawing the frontier between unilingual and bilingual France in his time. It is true that the thing would not have been as simple as we have made it sound: there are socio-linguistic situations where the shift from one form of speech to another does not seem to be sudden, but gradual. In certain sections of Picardy, before and during the Second World War, the linguistic situation could be characterized as follows: when first confronted with strangers, civil servants, holiday-makers from Paris, and the like, local peasants would use a sort of local French close enough to the average, if not to the standard form, to be generally understood. This, they would even use for a time among themselves in the presence of strangers, but very soon features from their dialect$_2$ would begin to crop up: *était, mangeait* would gradually yield before /eto/, /mãʒo/ with the local /-o/ ending in the imperfect; French vocabulary items would persist a little longer, but eventually such a form as *chaussette*, pronounced locally as [ʃoseât] (in dialect₁), would be replaced by the regular Picard /køʃɛt/. The outcome would be a form of speech generally impervious to anyone except the initiated. This type of stratification suggests the possibility of a gradual word-by-word and form-by-form elimination of dialect₂ through stages where different styles would coexist just as they do, for instance, in unilingual French. Such a type may have been, or may still be, fairly general along the periphery of the Paris Basin, but it is by no means the necessary intermediate step between dialect₂ situations and unilingualism, since a sudden break is just as likely.

Dialectal bilingualism in its neater form, i.e. one with clearly distinct dialect₁ and dialect₂, deserves to be dwelt upon a little further, since professional dialectologists, who are mostly antiquaries looking for old forms in any context (dialect₁ or dialect₂), have not been inclined to describe the socio-linguistic settings in which they operate.

The illustrations that follow are based upon observations carried out in Franco-Provençal territory, more precisely in Savoy, a region where dialects₂ were doomed as the result of the contacts established in the course of the First World War. Although we shall use here the present tense, the situation referred to is, generally speaking, that which prevailed at the eve of that war. Dialect₁ is, with careful speakers, a fairly good approximation to average French, closer probably than in most unilingual rural regions. This largely results from the fact that people are aware that what is good for dialect (dialect₂) is not good for French; French, of course, is taught at school, and school attendance is universal. Only very few, usually feeble-minded, old women speak only dialect₂ although they understand spoken French (dialect₁).

Dialect₂ is a variety of that type of Romance called Franco-Provençal whose domain, limited by Provençal in the south and merging gradually into the Burgundian and Franc-Comtois areas in the north, spreads from the upper

Loire valley in the west to the Schwyzer Tütsch area in the east. It is still a matter of dispute how and when this particular segment of the Romance-speaking area acquired the measure of autonomy which must be postulated by anyone who has discovered, behind the motley of contemporary patois, a bundle of fundamental likenesses. Dialect$_2$ varies from village to village, at times from hamlet to hamlet, and its use secures unimpeded communication within a radius of 10 to 15 miles at best. Beyond that distance, peasants may find it easier to use French (dialect$_1$). In a period of increasing division of labour and geographic mobility, this means that dialect$_2$ is doomed: people speak French better and better and are never given a chance to eliminate pre-existing or developing variations among dialects$_2$; the range of forms and words that are understood and used if necessary, constantly decreases: at Hauteville,[1] former generations accepted for 'bull' the form /bŏr'ră/ beside the local /tŏ're/; younger people who speak French with those for whom /bŏr'ră/ is the normal dialect$_2$ form never get acquainted with it. Had both parties tried to converse in dialect$_2$, both forms would have retained their wider currency. As a matter of fact, any reference to a bull among people from the /bŏr'ră/ and the /tŏ're/ zones will, from then on, be made by means of French *taureau* pronounced locally (dialect$_1$) [tɔ'ro] (as against Parisian [toʁo]). It might be advantageous to reserve in technical parlance the word 'patois' for the designation of minimal linguistic communities limited to a few thousands and even a few hundreds of rural speakers. But since, then, no patois situation is likely to endure, it may not be advisable to keep a word for such a transient phenomenon.

Dialect$_1$, alias local French, contains permanent and universal deviations from average or standard French, most, but not necessarily all, of them carried over from dialect$_2$: *aller en*

---

[1] Cf. A. Martinet, 'Description phonologique du parler franco-provençal d'Hauteville (Savoie)', *RLiR*, xv, pp. 1–85, revised and reprinted in *La Description phonologique avec application au parler franco-provençal d'Hauteville (Savoie)* (Geneva, 1956).

champs les vaches 'grazing the cattle', for standard *faire paître les bœufs*, *quand moi* 'when I did', for standard *'en même temps que moi*, *pôche* 'ladle', (dialect$_2$ /ˈpoθĕ/) for standard *louche*, &c. Most of these are normally used by both unilingual dialect$_1$ speakers (teachers and priests, for instance) and bilinguals. But, at any time, dialect$_2$ forms may, in the speech of the latter, be transferred to dialect$_1$ with just the necessary phonological and morphological adaptations. Children who pride themselves on their early handling of the standard language are particularly apt to effect this type of transfer: as a calque of dialect$_2$ [aˈbadda ˈbjɛ· le ˈplo·tə pə kã·ˈbɔ· lə gɔˈʎa], approximately 'take a big step to get over the puddle', a ten-year-old girl said once: *Abade bien les plotes pour camber le goillat* [abad bjẽ le plɔt pur kãbe l gɔja], the phonology of which was that of dialect$_1$ (local French), the grammatical cement and the adverb *bien* were average and standard French, but where the four lexemes *abade*, *plote*, *cambe*, and *goillat* were exclusively local. The closest standard French equivalent would have been *Écarte bien les jambes pour enjamber la flaque*. It should be pointed out that this utterance, when heard, excited the merriment and the derision of the by-standers, with some comment to the effect that if the girl could not speak French better, she had better use the patois which she would have handled to the general satisfaction. What deserves particular consideration here is, however, less the extent to which a bilingual person may let one language influence the other, than the fact that the sentence with its local lexicon is readily and unmistakably identified as French, ludicrous French indeed, but French, and not the local vernacular, because the phonology and the grammatical monemes are those of dialect$_1$, not dialect$_2$.

It would be interesting to determine whether some local words such as *abader*, *plote*, *camber*, and *goillat* survive to date in the speech of ten-year-old children who, in the regions concerned, are by now definitely French unilinguals. If some do, it probably will not be for long.

The process of dialect₂ elimination we have sketched above has certainly not yet affected the whole of Romance-speaking France, but it cannot be doubted that unilingualism is establishing itself in more and more rural districts at the expense of Provençal, Languedoc, Gascon, Catalan, and Corsican dialects. As regards Catalan and Corsican, it is often felt that their status differs from that of Gallo-Romance dialects because, diachronically speaking, they belong together with Hispanic and Central Italian Romance respectively. What may count, socio-linguistically, is the fact that the use of Catalan and Corsican dialects enables some Frenchmen to establish linguistic contacts with foreigners with whom French is no recourse, i.e. people who do not have French as a common, official language. Inasmuch as these contacts across the Spanish border or the Tyrrhenian Sea are lively and profitable, they may retard or prevent the crumbling down of the dialects in question into a multitude of mutually hardly intelligible patois, the prelude to their eventual elimination. To what extent contacts across the border do consolidate the Catalan dialects spoken on French territory and make them more resistant to the disintegrating pressure of the official language than their Languedoc or Gascon neighbours, remains to be investigated. In the case of Corsica, distance and the lack of territorial contiguity may largely contribute to the conservation of the vernaculars. In those margins of France where non-Romance forms of speech are in common use, the possibility of using them for contacts, across the border, with people who do not speak French must also be reckoned with as an asset for the vernacular. This undoubtedly plays a role in the case of Basque, with a majority of Euzkarian speakers on the Spanish side of the Pyrenees and a lively intercourse from north to south, particularly in the region close to the Bay of Biscay. Breton, spoken exclusively on its land's end by people who all learn French at school, does not find any support outside and must be receding rapidly, even on the rural front, in spite of the

gallant efforts of a handful of mostly French-speaking intel-
lectuals. Flemish should, in principle, stand a good chance
of resisting the pressure of French, since its French domain
is nothing but a fringe of a large area including north-western
Belgium and the Netherlands. Yet as long as French remains
a prestige language among the Belgian bourgeoisie of West
Flanders, the Flemish dialects of France cannot withstand the
pressure of the official language. The Alsatian situation, which
also applies to the northern stretches of Lorraine, is, in fact,
trilingual, with German dialects as vernaculars, and two competing national languages, the former official language,
German, still extensively used by the Churches and in part of
the press, and French, which is by now the universal teaching
medium in schools. Both German and French could be said
to be used under the form of dialects$_1$. The local dialects$_2$
are widely divergent, which would seem to bear witness to an
early use of a common standard, namely German, but their
position does not seem to be really threatened so far.

What seems decisive for the comportment of speakers of a
local form of speech in conflict with a standard language is
less, as generally imagined, the degree of similarity or dis-
similarity of their structure and vocabulary, than whether
the standard language is the same for all the speakers of a
given vernacular or whether the vernacular is felt as a link
with people who could not be reached through the language
one is taught at school and trained in in the army. Accordingly, the socio-linguistic situation should be much the same
in Romance Gascony and Celtic Brittany, differences in
sentimental reactions notwithstanding.

The preceding rapid survey of linguistic variety in France
would not be complete unless something were said of the
language situation in the French West Indies, a few islands
which are, politically, a part of Metropolitan France. Their
population, predominantly African in origin, are taught
standard French at school, but normally speak among themselves what is dubbed a French Creole, namely a form of

speech whose lexicon is essentially French, but whose morpho-syntax is very peculiar and clearly redolent of African linguistic habits. The phonology is also definitely in keeping with many features observable in languages of western Africa.[1] This type of situation is, of course, known elsewhere: there are English, Dutch, and Portuguese as well as French Creoles, the morpho-syntax of all of which evince a number of strikingly similar features.[2] Linguists have been debating the problem of whether a French Creole should be considered a Romance or an African form of speech, and in view of the overwhelming Frenchness of the vocabulary, the latter point of view sounds very much like a paradox.[3] Yet if we insist on labelling as French the sentence *abade bien les plotes pour camber le goillat*, where the lexemes are Franco-Provençal, just on account of the use of French phonology and grammatical items, we might argue that we could call a Creole an African dialect. What is decisive, however, on a pragmatic level, is the fact that the *abade bien* . . . utterance was meant to be French, and only the fact that the speaker had such a limited command of French lexicon prevented it from being universally acceptable as such. In the case of Creole, any utterance is meant to be Creole and nothing else, whatever the origin of the various ingredients may be. It is never supposed to be Ewe or Wolof with a French lexicon. Little advantage would be derived from attempts to force the very specific Creole situation into moulds previously established by comparativists. From a synchronic standpoint, it differs from any situation observed in Continental France in the sense that no vernacular there combines so much similarity on the lexical level with such very different syntactic habits. There is little doubt that if schooling were as thorough

---

[1] Cf. the thesis of Suzanne Sylvain, *Le Créole haïtien* (Wetteren, 1936).
[2] Best shown by Beryl Loftman in an unpublished Columbia University M.A. dissertation in 1953.
[3] Cf. the debate in *Word*, with Douglas Taylor, Robert A. Hall, Jr., and Uriel Weinreich as participants, xii (1956), pp. 407–14; xiv (1958), pp. 367–79; xv (1959), pp. 485–9.

in Martinique and Guadeloupe as it is in the department of Basses-Pyrénées, Creole users would achieve a complete mastery of French far more easily than their Euzkarian fellow citizens.

The widespread belief in the unity and homogeneity of the language of a given 'community' does not only conceal the linguistic variations existing within the boundaries of each state, but tends to convince even the educated that the language people speak and the language they write is necessarily the same. This is, in some cases, palpably untrue, and, in others, open to question. When a linguistic community, illiterate hitherto, gets acquainted with the art of writing, this is used for the rendering of some other language. In such a case, dissociating the writing from the language requires a power of abstraction that may be absent, so that the first persons who write do so in the foreign language. This may become institutionalized, so that literate people go on speaking their vernacular, sometimes exclusively, and do not know how to write except in another language. In many cases, the written language is that of a 'classical' literature or that of a liturgy, which was the case with Latin in medieval Europe, and is still so with Sanskrit in India and Koran Arabic in Muslim countries. This, it is true, is not always exclusive of efforts to apply writing to the vernaculars. But, as a rule, those efforts take centuries to bear appreciable results.

It could be objected that the fact that some people use a foreign or ancient language as a written medium is a very special case and that it does not mean that the written language of a nation is necessarily different from its spoken medium. Most people would concede, however, that there may be, between one and the other, a difference of style: the chief reason why people do not write as they speak is probably that since writing leaves permanent traces, whereas speech, unless recorded, is lost for ever, writers are far more careful than speakers: everybody would say things he would never dare put on paper. Consequently, written style is not spoken style. But it is not always easy to distinguish, here, between style and language: did Gregory of Tours, when he wrote his *Historia francorum*, some time in the second half of the sixth century, use a learned style of his own language, or another language? We shall be tempted to speak of one and the same language as long as the different linguistic forms are felt to be complementary because each situation requires one definite form and excludes all others, so that the user will never be faced with the necessity of making a decision as to what form to choose. No one will hesitate to speak of different styles if there actually is at the user's disposal a whole gamut of different linguistic forms merging gradually into one another, as is practically the case with the contemporary national languages in which anything can be found in print, with a tendency for frontiers between genres to get blurred.

It is often said that some difference between spoken language and written language is rendered inevitable because so many decisive features of speech are not transferred to writing. Whereby people mean the accentual hierarchy, so imperfectly rendered by the occasional use of italics, intonation, whose salient features only may be suggested by our punctuation, and all those peculiarities that characterize individual elocution. This amounts to saying that writing, with print as its ideal form, is a set of discrete visible symbols, each corresponding to some discrete audible unit of speech, and anything that is not discrete will be sacrificed in the transfer. There is a large measure of truth in this: in the last analysis, many of the features that differentiate written style from spoken style can be traced back to a need, in writing, to compensate for the loss of suprasegmental and individual elements of speech. Through too much insistence on the blurring of contextual features, however, one is apt to forget, or at least to minimize, the importance of situation in spoken communication, and the necessity to compensate for its absence in writing: a speaker may at all times refer to what he has, *hic et nunc*, in common with the hearer; the author has nothing in common with the reader but his text, and the fact that they belong to the same linguistic community. It will not do to argue that the author constantly re-creates situations so that he will use 'shifters',[1] words that are understood in situation only, like *I, you, here, last year*, just as easily when he writes as when he talks. The very fact that he has to recreate his situations if he wants to make use of a large part of the lexicon suggests that an appreciable part of his activity is devoted to descriptions and presentations from which 'shifters' are excluded except when, quite exceptionally, the author ('I') addresses his readers ('you'). As a matter of fact, contemporary literature has done much to introduce spoken style in written matter: the ideal of some writers is obviously to try to do away with presentations and descriptions and to let their characters 'speak for themselves'. But the difference between written style and spoken style is not thereby wiped out: they speak in print, instead of speaking aloud, and the ideal of a written style, self-sufficient, relying exclusively on discrete, linguistically central, non-expressive elements, survives, less perhaps in literature in the narrow sense of fiction, than in philosophical and scientific writings.

The distinction between literary language, or style, and colloquial speech is, of course, not identical with that between primary spoken form and secondary written form, as our use of 'written' and 'spoken' style may have suggested: contractions like *don't, can't, ain't* belong to various levels of 'spoken' style; still, they have a written form, and the many words that are hardly used outside of written texts have a pronunciation of their own, if only because they may have to be read aloud. Still, there are a few words that are so definitely spoken rather than written that there is no tradition governing their spelling; such is French /pagaj/, 'mess',

---

[1] So called by Otto Jespersen, *Language, Its Nature, Development, and Origin* (London, 1922), pp. 123–4.

which, in print, may appear as *pagaye, pagaïe,* or *pagaille;* popular German /ˈfuzel/, 'spirit', cannot even be given a suitable written form, since *Fusel,* which is found in dictionaries, would correspond to */ˈfūzəl/ and *Fussel* to */ˈfusəl/. The reverse is far more common: hosts of English words are so generally learnt through print that no single pronunciation can permanently establish itself (*gerrymander* with [g] or with [dʒ]?).

In a comparison of the frequently distinct systems presented by the written form and the spoken form of one and the same language, one may, in order to make the contrast the more striking, combine in one pattern the archaisms of the spelling and those of the literary style on the one hand, the innovations of the spoken form and those of colloquial speech on the other hand. As an illustration of how profoundly different things can be subsumed under a single language label, the case of French may be dealt with at some length.

English spelling gives, in many respects, a less reliable picture of the spoken form than French does: it is bad enough for native speakers who have to discover that what they pronounce /red/ is either *red* or *read*; it is a frightful nuisance for foreigners who have to pronounce *read* sometimes as /riˑd/, sometimes as /red/; but it does not give an inaccurate picture of the main lineaments of spoken grammar. French spelling gives foreigners fairly reliable hints as to how to pronounce vowels; where it is under-differentiated (/a/ or /ɑ/, /e/ or /ɛ/, and the like), Frenchmen as a whole do not really care about differentiation in speech. The real trouble is for Frenchmen who waste the best years of their childhood trying to figure out when they shall be content with the bare stem or when they shall write -*s,* or -*nt,* or -*t.* Formerly, those children who went to school had to learn grammar as a preparation for Latin lessons to come. In the world of today, where hundreds of millions of children go to school with no intention of ever learning Latin, grammar, a highly abstract affair, perfectly unsuited for the budding intellect of the average ten-year-old youngster, is doomed as a universal prerequisite. French children, however, will have to go on carrying the old burden as long as they have to decide when /iʃãt/ is to be spelled *il chante* and when *ils chantent*.

What follows is a sketch of the verbal forms of French in what could be designated as 'unguarded' spoken usage.[1] This, in turn, may vary from one region to another, and what will be considered specifically is the type of speech observable among people living in Paris. But it must be understood that this type has a much wider currency and that speakers of all provinces tend to conform to it. Some of the forms below may, in their written garb, strike one as extremely vulgar and belonging to a popular rather than a familiar level. Yet all of them can be heard in the speech of all social classes. They are normally used by the present writer in his home.

Some forms that have been disregarded cannot be said to be totally absent in informal conversations: the present writer, even in his most slipshod linguistic behaviour, may well be pushed into risking an imperfect subjunctive in a cascade of subordinate clauses. But he will hate himself for being tricked into it, since he is just as likely to use a wrong /-s/ form in the third person singular as the right, /-s/-less form. As a matter of fact, our examination will be restricted to those forms which adult speakers of any social class know how to use and use without tremor.

By 'verbal forms', we mean the set or sets of verbal *signifiants*, with their variants, that children have to learn before they can handle the language in a way that will satisfy their elders. Therefore it is not our intention to dwell here on compound forms as distinct from their components, the auxiliary on the one hand, the participle and the infinitive on the other. French, just like, and even more than, English, has a host of compound forms, even if we disregard quasi-

---

[1] For a fuller treatment of the same, see 'De l'économie des formes du verbe en français parlé' in *Studia philologica et litteraria in honorem L. Spitzer* (Berne, 1958), pp. 309–26.

modal combinations such as *il doit aller, il peut faire*, and the
like. The most striking development in this respect is the
spread of doubly compound forms such as (*quand*) *il a été parti*
or *il avait eu pris*, whose ultimate source must have been the
necessity of distinguishing between the true perfect with a
present meaning, as in *quand j'ai fini*, and the compound past,
quand j'ai eu fini, built from the former on the analogy of *j'ai
faim*, a present with, as a corresponding past, *j'ai eu faim*. Any
study of the syntactic functioning of the verbal system will
have to place such a form as *j'ai eu fini* among the constitutive
elements of that system. But, for us here, it is nothing but a
present form *ai* and two past participles *eu* and *fini*.

Before we pass on to the analysis of our forms, the problem
of linkings (*liaisons*) had better be dealt with apart. French
verbal endings are felt to be particularly tricky because,
according to whether the next word begins with a vowel or a
consonant, a characteristic *liaison* consonant may be sounded
or not. This is quite true for any sort of 'guarded' French
which is to some extent affected by the spelling. But in the
informal style we are considering here post-verbal linkings
have been preserved only in some very specific situations, so
that they should no longer be considered formal variations
of the verbal forms, but parts of variant forms of certain pronouns. Most post-verbal linkings that are suggested by the
spelling are either fanciful or optional and actually exceptional in familiar delivery: pronouncing a /-z-/ in *tu donnes à*
. . . would sound ridiculous although the *liaison* is acceptable
after sg. 2 in the case of the copula and a few very common
verbs: contrast, for *tu es une* . . . 'guarded' /tyɛzyn/, familiar
/tyɛyn . . ./, and slipshod /tɛyn/; *ils donnent une* . . . is /idɔnyn
. . ./, just like *il donne une* . . ., or /ildɔntyn . . ./ in careful
speech; the desire to distinguish between sg. 3 and pl. 3 undoubtedly contributes to making the /-t/ linking here more
frequent than the /-z/ linking of sg. 2: in the same style we
may hear /-t/ linking in *ils donnent un livre*, but no linking in
les parents donnent un livre, where the plurality of the subject

is previously indicated. Yet other factors intervene which restrict the use of /-t/ after pl. 3: a linking would sound queer, even in careful speech, in *ils contribuent à* . . . (/ilkõtribya . . ./, hardly / . . . byta . . ./). In short, linking here is never obligatory as long as the following item is not a pronoun. If it is a pronoun in subject function, it is necessarily a third person pronoun (*il, ils, elle, elles, on*), and these are always preceded by a /-t-/, irrespective of whether its spelled equivalent is a regular part of the written word, as in *il part, part-il, ils donnent, donnent-ils*, or an *ad hoc* addition as in *donne-t-on*. Only imperatives may be followed by dependent pronominal complements, among which only *en* and *y* begin in the spelling with a vowel; as a matter of fact they are always preceded by /-z-/ irrespective of whether the imperative form is permanently spelled with -*s* (*cours, cours-y*) or not (*va, vas-y*). If we leave the spelling out of the picture, we may summarize all this as follows: the pronouns /i(l), i(lz), ɛl, ɛl(z), õ/ are pronounced /ti(l), ti(l), tɛl, tɛl, tõ/ when they stand after the verb (N.B. this is not common in current informal speech where interrogation is indicated by means of preposed /esk/, *est-ce que*, rather than by inversion); the pronouns /ã/, *en*, and /i/, *y*, are pronounced /zã/ and /zi/ when placed immediately after an imperative. Compulsory linkings being thus dealt with in the frame of the formal variation of pronouns, they can be disregarded in an analysis of familiar spoken French.

What we call 'ending' here is any segment of the verbal form that follows another segment identified as a radical. An ending may be further analysed into a succession of distinct monemes: the -*rais* /-rɛ/ of *chanterais* is an ending made up of /-r-/, which is found in future forms, and /-ɛ/, which is found in imperfects.

In the type of French we are considering here, the only moods and tenses we should operate with are the following:

1. The present, which we need not call 'present indicative' since it is, in informal French, the only present tense positively marked as such through its opposition to non-present tenses.

It is characterized by a zero ending in sg. 1, 2, 3 and pl. 3, /-õ/ in pl. 1 and /-e/ in pl. 2. Informal French, however, normally employs pl. 1 forms with a zero ending and /õ/ as the subject pronoun: /õ dɔn/ *on donne*, instead of /nu dɔnõ/, *nous donnons*, with /nu õ dɔn/, *nous, on donne*, as an insistent form. Here is the resulting paradigm:

ʒ dɔn	õ dɔn
ty dɔn	vu dɔn-e
i dɔn	i dɔn

2. The imperfect, which we need not call 'imperfect indicative' since we do not reckon with any other imperfect. It is characterized by an /-ɛ/ ending in sg. 1, 2, 3, pl. 3, and informal pl. 1. The endings are /-iõ/ for less informal pl. 1 and /-ie/ for pl. 2. Hence the following paradigm:

ʒ dɔn-ɛ	õ dɔn-ɛ
ty dɔn-ɛ	vu dɔn-ie
i dɔn-ɛ	i dɔn-ɛ

3. The future which is marked by a combination of /-r-/ plus a vowel which is /-e/ or /-ɛ/[1] for sg. 1, /-a/ for sg. 2, 3, and informal pl. 1, /-õ/ for traditional pl. 1 and pl. 3, /-e/ for pl. 2. The ensuing paradigm

ʒ dɔn-rɛ	õ dɔn-ra
ty dɔn-ra	vu dɔn-re
i dɔn -ra	i dɔn-rõ

is etymologically connected and, perhaps, synchronically supported by that of the present of 'to have': /ɛ[2] a a a av-e õ/.

---

[1] Cf. *Prononciation*, pp. 122–6: among Parisian speakers, 53 per cent. rhyme *serai* with *été*; most of the rest rhyme it with *était*; the percentage for /-e/ sinks to 40 for the youngest third. Note that /-e/ is widely known to be the 'right' form.

[2] It would be worth while investigating to what extent the speakers who use /ɛ/ as the sg. 1 of the present of *avoir* are the same who pronounce future sg. 1 as /-rɛ/.

It might be tempting to assume that its comparative complexity has been instrumental in the promotion of compound futures of the *il va donner* /i va dɔne/ type. But it should be kept in mind that the present of the auxiliary *aller* is just as complex: /vɛ va va va al-e võ/.

4. The conditional, whose status as a tense or as a mood we need not discuss here. It is marked by /-r-/ followed by the endings of the imperfect. Hence:

ʒ dɔn-rɛ	õ dɔn-rɛ
ty dɔn-rɛ	vu dɔn-rie [dɔnərje]
i dɔn-rɛ	i dɔn-rɛ

When it is used as the future in the past (*il disait qu'il donnerait* 'he said he would give') it is often replaced by a compound form parallel to *il va donner* (*il disait qu'il allait donner*), but the /-r-/ form is indispensable as the conditional proper: *il donnerait cher pour.* . . .

5. The subjunctive, which corresponds to the present subjunctive of traditional grammars. Its marks are zero for sg. 1, 2, 3, informal pl. 1 and pl. 3, /-iõ/ and /-ie/ for less informal pl. 1 and for pl. 2 respectively. The informal paradigm

ʒ dɔn	õ dɔn
ty dɔn	vu dɔn-ie
i dɔn	i dɔn

is identical with that of the present with the exception of pl. 2. Only such verbs as make use of different stems for present and subjunctive manage to keep the two tenses distinct throughout. The subjunctive is actually in most cases what has been called a 'grammatical servitude': its use is largely restricted to certain grammatical contexts from which other tenses are excluded: after *il faut que*, *vous donnez* and *vous donnerez* are excluded; the subjunctive form *vous donniez* is compulsory and consequently does not contribute any information. But children learn frequent forms like *je sois, je fasse* very early, so that these survive after young speakers have learnt to use analogy, and the subjunctive shows few signs of obsolescence.

6. The imperative has only three distinctive forms, those of sg. 2, pl. 1 and 2, with zero, /-õ/ and /-e/ respectively, i.e. the same endings as the present. Traditional pl. 1 imperatives in /-õ/ seem seriously affected by the disaffection for such forms: traditional *chantons*, 'let's sing', is likely to be replaced in many situations by such phrases as *allez! on chante* or *allons! on chante*, in which the status of *allons* is close to that of an interjection.

The non-personal moods present three distinct forms: those of the infinitive, the present participle, and the past participle. The present participle is always in /-ã/, but the infinitive and the past participle have endings that vary from one type to another: most of the verbs that present the same stem throughout have /-e/ for both (/dɔn-e/); those that add their personal endings to different stems end their infinitives in /-r/ (/fini-r/, /bat-r/), but in the case of such verbs as *devoir*/dvuar/ or *partir*/partir/, we may either decide that the ending is just /-r/ and the infinitive stems are /dvua/ and /parti/ distinct from both /dua/, /par/ of *je dois je pars*, and /dv-/, /part-/ of *vous devez, vous partez*, or posit that the infinitive endings are /-uar/ and /-ir/ respectively, the stems being in that case those of present pl. 2 /dv-/ and /part-/. Past participles of verbs with /-r/ infinitives may either be said to end in zero (/fini/; cf. /ʒ fini/), in /-i/ (/part-i/; cf. /ʒ par/) or in /-y/ (/bat-y/; cf. /ʒ ba/), or be all of them considered bare stems (/parti/, /baty/, just like /fini/).

But the infinitive and the participles are, of course, quasi-nominal forms that stand aside from properly conjugated ones. The past participle and the infinitive are in French so frequent that children often learn them as if they were independent words with no formal allegiance to the personal moods. This accounts for the fact that obsolescent French verbs are as a rule verbs which people do not know how to conjugate, but whose infinitive and past participle are remembered and used if necessary.

If, in consequence, we dissociate conjugated from non-conjugated forms and concentrate on the former, we may summarize our observations by saying that in spoken colloquial French all verbs are inflected in the same way, i.e. by means of the addition of the same endings to a stem, but that whereas most verbs, such as *je donne* (/ʒ dɔn/), present the same stem throughout, others distinguish between a short stem (e.g. /ʒ ba/) and a long stem (/vu bat-e/), others still, among those with the highest frequency, presenting short stems and different long stems with peculiar distributions (e.g. /ʒ vɛ/, /ty va/, /ʒ i-rɛ/, /vuz al-e/, /ʒ aj/, for *aller*). Such isolated remnants as /nu sɔm/ *nous sommes* or /vu fɛt/ *vous faites*, where it made sense to identify an /-m/ ending and a /-t/ ending as long as the simple past, with its regular /-m/ and /-t/ endings in pl. 1 and 2 (/nuz ala-m/ *nous allâmes*, /vuz ala-t/ *vous allâtes*) was part of the system, must, in the frame of contemporary colloquial French, be considered unanalysable amalgams.

The picture is completely different if we consider now literary French in its written form. There is probably little need here to list forms that can all be found in any grammar of French. Two tenses, the simple past and the imperfect subjunctive, that have been disregarded in the preceding survey, re-enter the picture, and thereby the connexion between the quasi-nominal items and the conjugated form is largely restored: *donné* is predictable from *je donnai*, *parti* from *je partis*, *couru* from *je courus*, and vice versa in spite of exceptions like *je cousis*, *cousu*. But the main difference lies in the fact that all verbs do not take the same endings: some take -*e*, -*es*, -*e* in the singular of the present indicative, while others take -*s*, -*s*, -*t*. It is therefore necessary to posit different conjugations, just as in Latin, Italian, or Spanish, and this is actually what we find in traditional grammars; irrespective of whether grammarians decide to list two of them, if they start from the present indicative, or more than two if the infinitive, the form under which the verb is quoted, is taken as a starting-point. Among these conjugations, one is said to be productive, the one with endings in -e- (-e, -es, -e, -er, &c.). It corresponds roughly to the one-stem verbs of spoken colloquial French. This coincidence between productivity and invariability of the stem is, of course, not fortuitous: a denominative like *canoter* from *canot* or a loan like *dribbler* from English *dribble* cannot be expected to modify its stem, unless the modification is somehow automatic and consequently predictable; e.g./ʒ dribl/ with the stem pronounced as [dʀibl], future /ʒ dribl-rɛ/ pronounced [dibʀləʀɛ]. But this does not lessen the contrast between the two systems, one with distinct conjugations, the other with a single conjugation, but a distinction between those verbs whose forms can all be predicted if any one of them is known, and those for which this is not the case.

Two so fundamentally different systems can be made to coexist as two styles of the same language only through a painful and protracted training, which a nation will impose on all its new members when it is felt that thereby a precious cultural heritage will be preserved. This is not the place to discuss whether the burden could be lessened without affecting that heritage, for instance through some drastic spelling reform. Our only aim in presenting the two systems was to illustrate how different two linguistic forms that purport to be 'the same language' can be.

V

LINGUISTIC EVOLUTION

IT is customary, among contemporary descriptivists, to consider that pre-structural linguistics dealt exclusively with the history of languages. This is not quite accurate: traditional linguistics, as practised during the last 150 years, has probably more often been engaged in comparing genetically related languages and trying to account for some feature of one by reference to some features of another, than in trying to determine how and why a given language had evolved through the centuries. In other words, scholars have been more inclined to point out correspondences than to explain them. It is true that no serious research can be pursued that is not based upon observation; history implies the study of documents, and, even for the best known among languages, our documentation is full of gaps. Therefore, it may have been scientifically safer in many instances to avoid historical treatments altogether.

Actually, most linguists, until the dawn of structural linguistics, were not aware of any necessity of distinguishing between diachrony and synchrony, and, quite frequently, they studied what Saussure called *états de langue* without drawing any clear boundary between comparative attempts and diachronic references on the one hand, and synchronic observation on the other hand.

Today, after decades of conscious synchronic practice, it is certainly easier to understand what historical linguistics really implies. On the plane of general linguistics, it amounts to determining how and why languages change through time, and this is what is meant here by linguistic evolution.

This problem was at one time a favourite with some language theorists, but mainly as far as sound changes were in question. Sober scholars, in spite of their reluctance to enter the realm of hypotheses, had had to make up their minds regarding the nature of phonetic changes, and, in order to reach a decision, they had been compelled to consider the problem of how the obvious, if not total, regularity of sound changes could be explained. This regularity, whose reason is obvious as soon as speech is found to be analysable in terms of a definite number of discrete units, the phonemes, was for several decades the subject of strenuous debates, which resulted in its being generally acknowledged, at least as a working hypothesis. But since speech sounds were at that time usually considered not to belong to language proper, people were tempted to look for causes of change that lay outside of language, and preferably outside of man; hence the ever-recurrent references to climate, latitude, altitude, and the like.

We have now identified the outward manifestation of language as a perfectly legitimate part of it, and consequently we are not inclined to account for its vagaries in any other way than the one we shall use for other linguistic changes. It would seem that if languages change, as we know they do, it is, basically, because the needs of their users change, and this has been found to apply to phonology as well as to lexicon, morphology, or syntax. This, of course, involves a total revision of traditional views regarding sound changes.

Another basic contribution of contemporary research to the problem of linguistic change is the establishment of a relation between the frequency of a linguistic unit and its form, so that a change in frequency may involve a change in its phonic aspect. This, a consequence of the theory of selective information, applies to units of both articulations, to phonemes as well as to monemes. It leads to the conclusion that since the rise in the frequency of a unit is nothing but a rise in the number of times that unit is used, any use of a linguistic unit contributes, even if only in an infinitesimal way, to an increase in its frequency. This automatically entails a lowering of its contribution to information and a tendency to reduce its cost, that is the output of energy it requires for its memorizing and production. Such a reduction is likely to determine changes in the physical aspect of the unit. This could be summarized by saying that, strange as it may sound, a language changes because it is used.

People as a rule are not conscious of any change taking place in their language. When they are told and shown how different it was four or five centuries ago, they are apt to wonder how this came to pass and imagine some period of rapid change from one period of stability to another, the one they imagine they are enjoying. It is not difficult to understand the reasons of the common illusion that one's language is stable and homogeneous: people tend to identify language and its written form, and would naturally think that nothing changes as long as spelling has not budged; as a rule they do not and cannot remember how they spoke ten or twenty years before; everyone is used to and considers normal many forms and turns which he himself never uses, but which he seems always to have heard; he is likely to brand as 'accent' any deviation to which he is not used or which is so considered in his town or province; but as regards other features, his tolerance is boundless. This is all to the good; the chief aim of language is communication; it is greatly advantageous that on the one hand something that hampers communication should be resisted and denounced, and on the other hand that something that does not should be disregarded or condoned.

Yet no one will deny that under the pressure of technical advance the vocabulary of a language is likely to expand; most of us remember a period when *radar* and *sputnik* did not exist. We may also at times become conscious of the obsolescence of a word which was once of daily occurrence. But it is more difficult to imagine how the changing needs of man or his communities may influence the more intimate fabric of his language, namely the morphology and, above all, the phonology.

In order to understand how the influence of technical, economic, or cultural changes may spread to the inner core of language, we have to remember what we do when we want a linguistic communication to be more specific. If I want someone to pass me a certain book and if the request 'give me the book' does not make me get the desired object, I shall try to be more specific and say *give me the blue book* or *give me the blue book that lies on the far end of the shelf*. I might also replace *book* by another in itself more specific term like *octavo*. But it is far more usual to achieve specification through the addition of new elements to the sequence of meaningful units than by replacing one term by another. Besides, in the last analysis, a highly specific term like *octavo* is nothing but the residue of a phrase formerly used as a specification of *book* or some equivalent. People do not, as a rule, invent new monemes. All this is in keeping with the analytic process I have called the first articulation, according to which experience is subjected to an analysis manifested in linear form.

Now if my request had been presented in a very simple and somewhat primitive household, there would have been no need for any specification, because there would have been only one book there, namely the Bible or some almanac. But life having become more complex, people need more books and more specific books. On the plane of language, the result is that, while I might have got along in the past with a simple utterance made up of the injunctive *give* accompanied by two handy complements *me* and *the book*, the satisfaction of my needs will require now the addition of a relative clause and that of an attribute *blue*, which is an original predicate used here with the same function as that of a relative clause. It is thus clear that an increasing complexity of social relations will be accompanied by an increasing complexity of syntax. Division of labour will involve the appearance of new forms of human and material relations which will determine the appearance, in language, of new functions.

A language like Latin, considered in itself and in its evolution towards its modern Romance representatives, affords a fine illustration of how two types of function marking, corresponding to two successive periods in the evolution of the language, combined for a while, before the older type was eventually eliminated by the expansion of the more recent one: on the one hand, an inherited, formally rigid and strictly limited system of case-endings no longer capable of taking care of the expression of all the relations needed in Roman society; on the other hand, a set of former adverbs gradually promoted to the role of function marking prepositions constituting a very handy and expendable instrument, which, for a while, eked out the case system, but finally eliminated it as an unnecessary burden.

What this Latin example illustrates is not only the way increasing social complexity determines an expansion of the functional complexity of the corresponding linguistic medium, but also the protracted resistance of the language against the reorganization required by new social and communicative needs. Inertia combined with redundancy delays the spread to all the parts of the language structure of the repercussions of some initial change. As a result of this, a language is necessarily the battlefield of conflicting trends, the linguistic consequences of past social changes running against the implications of new innovations corresponding to new stages in the evolution of society and coming with them to terms which represent the structure of the language at every step. This implies that it is extremely difficult to trace linguistic causality back to its ultimate social antecedents. Linguists, once they have ascertained the decisive influence exerted by social factors on linguistic structure, should not try to do what they are not trained to do and what might lead them into the realm of unverifiable hypotheses, namely to examine the details of that influence and venture into the field of cultural history.

Their real task is to observe and describe, within a given

language and through a limited period, the various conflicts and trends in the frame of the permanent needs of human communication.

In order to understand how and why a language changes, the linguist has to keep in mind two ever-present and antinomic factors: first the requirements of communication, the need for the speaker to convey his message, and, second, the principle of least effort, which makes him restrict his output of energy, both mental and physical, to the minimum compatible with achieving his ends.[1] Now the objection is often raised that human activity in general, and linguistic activity in particular, may in many instances be an end in itself, a play: talking, more often than not, contributes very little to information; many people talk because they like it, not because they have anything to communicate. But this does not imply that linguistic evolution is not determined by the principle of least effort. Talking is often just a game, but a game is only worth while if he who plays the game sticks to the rules. Cheating makes sense only if the game ceases to be an end in itself, and there is, for chatterboxes, no reason why they should cheat in the game of talking. The rules of the game of speech are laid down by its communicative uses. At every stage, the structure of language is nothing but the unstable balance between the needs of communication, which require more numerous and more specific units, each of them of comparatively rare occurrence, and man's inertia, which favours less numerous, less specific, and more frequently occurring units. It is the interplay of these two main factors that constitutes the essentials of linguistic economy. We shall therefore concentrate on language as a communicative tool, since this use of language gives it a form likely to be imitated in all its other uses. We may thus posit, as the basic principle of language economy, that the amount of energy

---

[1] The basic treatment of least effort, also in reference to language, is still George K. Zipf's *Human Behavior and the Principle of Least Effort* (Cambridge, Mass., 1949).

spent toward linguistic ends will tend to be proportionate to the amount of information to be conveyed.

This might be construed as if no feature or unit in a language would endure unless it contributed to communication a share corresponding to the efforts required by its memorization and production. But this is palpably untrue; every language carries along a heavy load of most uneconomic forms which, for various reasons, have been retained throughout centuries. Some are learnt by children at an early age, before they are able to use analogy, when the language they use is so poor that its economy is bound to be very different from that of more-advanced users; others are forced upon us by reasons of prestige; others still are preserved because no indication is to be found anywhere as to how they could be adapted to current needs. But the main reason why the energy spent is not strictly proportionate to the amount of information intended by the speaker derives from the fact that communication hardly takes place in ideal situations; some amount of noise, man-made or not, interferes with the identification of the successive linguistic units by the audience; besides, people often listen intermittently because they rarely ascribe more importance to what is said to them than to their own latent or conscious preoccupations. Depending on various conditions, messages will be more or less repetitious, and this will be determinant for the average handling of language. Redundancy, in various forms, is a basic necessity of linguistic communication. As a matter of fact, human nature is such that a total elimination of redundancy might, in many circumstances, entail a serious increase of the energy spent on speech; as popular practice indicates, it is probably easier to use double or triple negatives (*I haven't seen nobody...*) than to order one's utterances in such a way that there should never be any repetition. Once the word *yesterday* figures in an utterance it is certainly less trouble to let the aura of past action pervade all that follows and determine the choice of past tense than to take advantage of the precise indication of the past contained in *yesterday* and dispense with tense endings. The more so, of course, if we have learned to do so as children.

Redundancy is indispensable for the transmission of language to new generations of speakers: a good many words are learned through identifying certain aspects of certain situations, say a given animal, the horse, with a certain vocal product. But thousands of others, which do not correspond to concrete objects or beings, are normally learned through redundant contexts, *hungry*, for instance, if learned by a child when listening to such utterances as *he's hungry; give him something to eat*, or *I'm hungry; when do we have dinner?* Learning new words through redundant contexts is a very common occurrence throughout life, whether this takes place in one's own or in some foreign language.

The importance of redundancy does not, of course, invalidate the concept of language economy, but reminds us of its complexity; what is easiest is not necessarily logically simplest. It would be totally erroneous to identify information meant and information actually conveyed.

All this means that linguists, in their efforts to understand how language changes, should undoubtedly take advantage of information theory, but that they should thereby keep in mind that, in any speculation involving cost, i.e. in our case, energy spent toward storage and production, or, if we prefer, memorization and actual use in speech, they will have to avoid attempts at mathematical formulation. There are two reasons for this: first and foremost, we have no way of quantifying that energy except in a very approximate fashion; we may point out, for instance, that, everything else being equal, the addition of a new phoneme to a succession of such entails the expenditure of extra energy: *feed* 'costs' more than *fee*. Secondly, even if we could achieve some quantification, other factors than the ones involved in information theory, factors which might, for instance, tie up with sociology, would remain so potent that we would not know what to do with our hard-won mathematical accuracy. Therefore, in language dynamics, we shall have to be satisfied with determining in what direction the variation of certain factors is likely to cause that of others. These variables are (1) the number of the units among which the speaker chooses at a given point in the utterance, (2) the probability of units, which we shall in practice identify with their frequency, either in a definite position or generally, (3) the cost of each unit, and (4) its information.

We call information whatever reduces uncertainty through the elimination of certain possibilities. This means that information is not the same as meaning. If I say *he has p*. . . . and stop short, *p* has, of course, no meaning, but it carries information because it excludes the possibility that the utterance may have been meant as *he has given* or *he has seen*. If I say *he has pr* . . ., *r* has no meaning, but, again, it contributes information because it eliminates *he has pushed* or *he has placed*. This implies that what is going to be said about the dynamics of language applies to all linguistic units, distinctive or significant, phonemes and monemes alike.

As is well known, the more numerous the units among which the speaker may choose, the more informative each of them will be: if someone is trying to locate a place on a map, and if, in my directions to him, I am only allowed to use the four cardinal points, telling him to look south will limit his research to one-fourth of the expanse; but, if I may also use compounds such as south-west and north-east, his research will be limited to one-eighth of the map. His uncertainty will thus be reduced, and we may say that each one of the directions in the eight-point system is more informative than each one in the cardinal, four-point, system.

Now if, in a certain place, the wind blows from the west just as often as from any other direction, the information contributed by *west* in reference to the wind will be that of each unit in a two-unit system; in other words, it will be smaller than if north, south, east, and west had been equally likely. This means that the information contributed by a unit depends on its probability in the context where it occurs. The more probable a unit, the less informative it is. The probability of a unit is presented in terms of frequency.

The relations between number of units or frequency of units on the one hand and information on the other hand follow, as it were, from the very definition of what information is. They are necessary and, should we say, automatic. If the frequency of an item decreases, its probability must necessarily decrease too, and nothing can prevent its information from soaring. The relationship between information and cost is of a totally different nature; if the information of a unit is affected either because of some increase or decrease in the number of units with which it is in competition, or because of some change in its frequency, we may expect that speakers will be tempted to let the output of energy in their production of that unit be partially determined by its new informational role. In other words, people will be ready to pay more for more information to be conveyed and inclined to pay less if information decreases. But it is by no means certain that they will, in all cases, be in a position to yield to that temptation: slurring, in case of a decrease in information, seems excluded as long as the unit in question, a word, for instance, is still in competition with a large number of similar units which have to be kept distinct. Only where the choice is limited to two or three possibilities, as when only *yes* or *no* can be expected, will the barriers raised by phonematic articulation crumble down, and grunts such as *uh-huh* take the place of a neat succession of distinctive units. If phonemes cannot be tampered with, the number of them may, in specific instances, be reduced through abbreviation, as when *professor* becomes *prof* and *underground railway, underground*, or through replacement, as when *tube* replaces *underground*. But there are cases and situations where, for various reasons, nothing can be done: it seems that, in America, no one has been able to find a handy and generally acceptable substitute for the comparatively frequent *elevator-operator*, and there are many situations where a professor is always a *professor* and never a *prof*. If, now, the information of a word increases, i.e. if its frequency diminishes, the bulk of its *signifiant* may well be preserved unchanged: the French for 'spinning-wheel' is still the three phoneme *rouet*, just as it was in the days when the word was in daily use, and this is likely to endure as long as no homonymic conflict arises.

Statistically, it seems true that, in all languages, the sum of the phonematic segments needed for the 500 most frequent words is smaller than that obtained for the next 500 lexical items; which means that frequent words are, on the average, shorter than rare words. But if the relationship between frequency and cost were of the same type as that between frequency and information, we should be able to state that, for a given frequency, a word should have *n* phonemes, no more and no less, and that a word of *n* phonemes should definitely belong to a given frequency range. This is, of course, not the case; *conspicuous* with its four syllables and eleven phonemes is so much more frequent than *dinosaur* with three syllables and seven phonemes. We have here a clear indication that a strictly mathematical treatment of the problems of language dynamics is not practicable. But the unmistakable existence of an inverse relationship between frequency and linguistic complexity is a most precious discovery.

This applies to all linguistic elements in so far as they convey information and to distinctive non-significant elements as well as to meaningful units, and it is perhaps advisable to illustrate this relationship, first by a reference to some phonological phenomena: the advantage of phonological illustrations lies in the fact that everything is so much simpler there, with a definite number of phonemes per language and no necessity to reckon with meaning. This would seem to outweigh the disadvantage resulting from the fact that many philologists feel more at ease among meaningful than among distinctive segments, among words than among phonemes.

It is quite likely that the different phonemes of a language are of different degrees of complexity, and that this should be taken into consideration when one tries to understand the dynamics of a phonological system.[1] But when dealing with phonological complexity it is easier and safer to look for it along the line of successivities and operate with the assumption that two successive phonemes require more energy than one. It is clear, on the other hand, that two successive phonemes give far more information than one: we get much closer to *I have praised* if we perceive, after *I have*, two phonemes /pr/ instead of just /p/. We come to the same conclusion if we start from /pr/ as a whole whose frequency we compare with that of, say, /p/. We may assume that, in a corpus of English utterances, there would be about twenty times as many /p/'s without a following /r/ than /pr/'s, which means that the information conveyed by /pr/ would be considerably higher. Therefore, it is worth while spending more energy on /pr/ than on /p/. Now, let us assume that, for some reason or other, the frequency of /pr/ increased so as to become equal or comparable with that of /p/. Speakers would certainly be tempted to reduce the amount of energy devoted to the production of /pr/ and make it similar to the one used for /p/. But dropping /r/ would not do, because /pr/ and /p/ would then be confused and, on account of the high frequency of both, misunderstandings would be so frequent, that speakers who, in principle, want to be understood, would correct themselves at once, so that /pr/ would never get a chance to be reduced. A reduction could only take place if either /p/ or /pr/ could be induced to become something else without creating conflicts: if /p/ could, for instance, become /f/ without conflicting with any previous labial fricative, then /pr/ could become /p/ without creating any confusion.

Now a sudden spate of /pr/'s is something I have never heard mentioned in any language at any stage of its evolution.

---

[1] Cf. G. K. Zipf, *The Psychobiology of Language* (Cambridge, Mass., 1935) and *Économie*, pp. 132–8.

Yet cases of rapid proliferation of some consonant clusters are on record in the case of the so-called 'geminates', i.e. the same consonant at the end and at the beginning of two successive syllables.

In modern English, geminates do not exist except at the juncture of two words, as in *pen-knife* /pen-naif/ or *head-dress*. But in many languages, such as Italian, Hungarian, or Finnish, geminates are perfectly normal within the same moneme. Geminates do not seem to have existed in what is reconstructed as Proto-Indo-European. But they were a normal feature of ancient Greek, Latin, and the older Celtic and Germanic languages. It seems that, at some time or other, the speakers of every one of these developed a habit of replacing single intervocalic consonants by geminates in words felt to be 'expressive':[1] the word *knock*, for instance, attested in Old English as *cnocian* with a single *c*, appears in Middle English as *knokke*, with a geminate which accounts for the quality of the modern vowel (from *cnocian*, one would have expected **knoke* rhyming with *oak*). In the course of centuries, these geminates ceased to be optional, and, as shown by the ME. *knokke*, became perfectly normal features of the words where they appeared. When added to the bulk of the ones that had developed through various phonologically regular processes, their frequency became comparable to that of their simple counterparts. In other words, the information of intervocalic /-kk-/ became similar to that of intervocalic /-k-/. In English, as in the other Germanic languages, the burden of the distinction between /-kk-/ and /-k-/ was generally shifted over to the preceding vowel: OE. *socian* became ME. *soke*, with the vowel lengthened, hence NE. *soak* with /oᵘ/, while ME. *knokke* preserved its short vowel, hence the non-diphthongized vowel of NE. *knock*. The distinction between /-kk-/ and /-k-/ could then disappear and the balance between information and cost be restored. It is interesting

---

[1] Cf. A. Martinet, *La Gémination consonantique d'origine expressive dans les langues germaniques* (Copenhagen, 1937), pp. 29–44, 104–47.

to notice that at the time when these successive changes took place in England, the English as a nation had hardly any contacts with the bulk of users of other Germanic languages. This indicates that the adoption of that particular solution of the problem must have been determined by such general features of the language pattern as the phonematic build of words and the quantitative system of vowels which at the beginning of the second millennium after Christ must still have been largely similar throughout the Germanic domain.

In Latin, the proliferation of geminates had begun earlier,[1] at a time when word final vowels had not been reduced, as it was in Germanic when the process of readjustment started, and this difference in the general economy of word forms contributes to explain the divergent paths followed in this connexion by Romance and Germanic. The assumption that Gaulish, the linguistic substratum of most of Western Romance, had a finger in the pie cannot be ruled out: the main initial features of the consonantal evolution of Western Romance and Brythonic Celtic are so much alike that one is legitimately tempted to assume that Gaulish, another Celtic form of speech, as it was being displaced by Latin, was undergoing what has been called 'lenition', and lenition, a weakening of intervocalic consonants, would be nothing but the outcome of a situation where geminates had begun to be practically as frequent as their simple intervocalic counterparts. The Western Romance consonantal shift would accordingly be nothing but a reflex of a Celtic shift. Yet the structural conditioning of the Western Romance change must have been largely present in late Latin, and the Celtic influence may have been just the last straw.

The Western Romance outcome is a general simplification of the geminates, as a rule without any confusion with corresponding single consonants. In the case of stops and

---

[1] Cf. A. Graur, *Les Consonnes géminées en latin* (Paris, 1935), where the expansion of gemination, supposed to be a Proto-Indo-European phenomenon, is examined. On gemination in Romance and Celtic, see *Économie*, pp. 257–96.

fricatives, the geminate, when reduced, preserves its articulation: late Latin *totta* becomes French *toute*, whereas the single consonant is shifted: Latin *tota* yielding Spanish *toda*. Nasals and liquids, for which, in the absence of any opposition of voice, the conditioning was largely different, present divergent treatments which point to later evolution: Castilian has palatal reflexes of /-ll-/ and /-nn-/ and retains /-l-/ and /-n-/ with their old values; Portuguese shifted the former to /-l-/ and /-n-/, while Latin single /-l-/ and /-n-/ were eventually eliminated as segments, although the nasal tamber of /-n-/ and, possibly, the velar quality of /-l-/, must have been carried over to neighbouring vowels, as we see from *são*<*sanum*. French shifted the burden of the distinction on to the preceding vowel, whose quality differed according to whether it was in a former open or checked syllable (OFr. *pele* 'shovel' from Lat. *pala*, but *balle* from germanic *balla*, *sain* from *sanum*, but *pan* from *pannum*). This is, of course, parallel to what we have found for Germanic at a much later period. In the case of /-rr-/ versus /-r-/, the process of simplification is still at work in many quarters. In the case of French, the burden of the distinction could not, in this case, be shifted to the preceding vowel because many /-rr-/ were the reflexes of former /-tr-/ and /-dr-/, as in *pierre*, from *petra*, and *lierre* (<*l'ierre*), from *hed(e)ra*. Since /-tr-/ and /-dr-/ did not 'make position' in Latin, the preceding vowel was in an open syllable and was treated as such, hence the diphthongs of *pierre* and *lierre*. But since the vocalism preceding the geminated /-rr-/ in *pierre* was the same as that preceding the single /-r-/ of *fiere*, from *fera*, the burden of the distinction was left to the consonant. It remained there, in some form or another, in Parisian French, down to the seventeenth century, when /-rr-/ must have passed first to a long uvular *r* which affected the tamber of some of the preceding vowels: today the intervocalic consonant is the same in *marron* and *parer*, but most older Parisian speakers have /ɑ/ in the former, and /-a-/ in the latter.

As soon as phonological changes are considered within the frame of the language system, the whole of the consonantal evolution of early Western Romance appears as ultimately conditioned by the economical necessity of reducing the energy needed by the articulation of geminates to the amount compatible with their informative value. It is not meant hereby that other factors have not been at work. To say that the difference between the Castilian and the Portuguese treatment of /-ll-/ is due to chance would amount to stating that the factors that have determined its shift to /-λ-/ in one language, /-l-/ in the other have not been identified yet. In a number of cases where French deviates from its partners, the more intimate contacts of that language with Germanic forms of speech must have been at work; lengthening and diphthongization of accented vowels in open syllables seem to be good illustrations of these. But the diverging treatments are nothing but locally determined reactions to the unbalance deriving from the high frequency and low informational value of geminates.

The existence of an inverse relationship between frequency and linguistic complexity is abundantly illustrated on the plane of grammar.[1] Statistically first, when it is found that grammatical items, each of which is on the average incomparably more frequent than is the case with lexical items, are as a rule much shorter than the latter. Minimal complexity, for a moneme, would seem to amount to formal inexistence, and this indeed is what we find in the case of such grammatical functions as are marked by position: in languages with a subject, i.e. a formally characterized compulsory actualizer of the predicate, no normal complete statement can exist without one. This determines a maximal probability which reduces the information to zero. Of course the choice of a given subject among all the ones available and

[1] Cf. A. Martinet, 'Linguistique structurale et grammaire comparée', *Travaux de l'Institut de linguistique*, i (1956), pp. 7–21.

likely in the particular context may furnish a large amount
of information. But the presence of a subject as such affords
none whatsoever, and it is normal that it should not be positively marked by a specific speech segment or any formal
modification. Consequently, a zero ending for 'subject-case'
is what should be expected. We find a similar situation when
we consider the 'object'. The object is not quite as compulsory as the subject: *eat* is never without a subject, except in
the imperative, but it may appear without an object. Yet,
once a given 'transitive' verb is chosen by the speaker, the
only information furnished by the object as such results
from the fact that it might have been suppressed. But in
contexts where an object is actually found in 99 per cent. of
the cases, its information is close to nil if considered in its
object-function, and not as a specific choice among a variety
of lexical or pronominal items. It is, therefore, normal that
the most frequent type of object should not be marked by any
specific segment, provided it is kept distinct from the subject
by means of word order.

This indeed corresponds to what we find in a majority
of languages with subjects. But there is an exception that
certainly looms large for classical scholars, namely the positively marked nominatives and accusatives of classical Indo-
European languages. If we leave out the plural cases which
raise special problems, we may state that, with the exception
of some neuters, the accusative, which is the case of a majority
of verbal objects, ends in -*m*. The nominative, often identified
as the subject-case, ends in -*s* in the majority of masculine
and feminine nouns. If we oppose masculine and feminine to
neuter as animate opposed to inanimate, we may say that
animate nouns ending in stops and prehistoric vowels present
an -*s* nominative (Latin *pleb-s, civi-s, ficu-s*); others, which
have what is often called a zero ending, have a stem-final
consonant or an -*ā* which must be the reflex of vowel+'laryn-
geal', the latter probably some fricative continuant. This
points to a prehistoric stage were -*s* was preserved after stop

or vowel, but dropped after a continuant (hence Greek animate nouns with final -ηρ, -ων, -η ($< -\bar{a} < $*-eH)), and a previous stage when -*s* was the universal ending of the nominative of animate nouns.

Whether the preceding reconstruction is accepted or not, we are faced with the existence, in early Indo-European languages, of an -*s* nominative limited to the designation of beings or objects conceived as animate. This limitation suggests that in Proto-Indo-European this -*s* marked a function felt to be characteristic of animate creatures, namely that of acting, as opposed to the passivity of things. Such -*s* forms could hardly be subjects, i.e. forms used with the function of compulsory actualizer of a predicate, because the zero information of a subject as such would hardly be compatible with a formally existing indicator. All this points to -*s* as the mark of an ergative case, the case of the agent, which must have coexisted with a true nominative, the form of the noun used in order to introduce or 'nominate' a person or to present a creature or an object. This true nominative, being used outside of grammatically organized utterances, was in no definite relation to a predicate and had therefore no grammatical function properly so called. It must have been identical with the bare stem of the word and, as such, identical with the vocative which also corresponded to a use of the noun outside of grammatically organized utterances. In languages that make use of an ergative case for the agent,[1] it is frequent, if not universal, to find the bare stem used for the most obvious complement of the predicate; in an utterance corresponding to 'the woman is washing the linen', the woman, as the agent, will be a complement in the ergative, but the linen, as the 'most obvious complement', will be in the nominative. The nominative, here, is no longer the subject case, but the bare stem as used in non-grammatical

---

[1] Basque is an example; for an evaluation of the ergative construction in Basque, see the author's paper 'La Construction ergative et les structures élémentaires de l'énoncé', *Journal de psychologie normale et pathologique* (1958), pp. 377–92.

contexts: in a word-for-word translation, the equivalent of the former utterance would sound like *washing [of] (the) linen by (the) woman* or *linen washing by woman*. With intransitive predicates, 'the most obvious complement' is identical with what we call the subject: 'the man talks' is presented as *talking [of] (the) man* or *man talking*, where *man* is treated as the normally expected complement, and consequently presented without explicit mark of its function.

A similar situation must have existed at some stage of Proto-Indo-European: the bare stem was used out of context as a nominative properly so called and as a vocative and, with a grammatical function, as the most obvious complement corresponding to the direct object of our transitive and the subject of our intransitive verbs; the -*s* form was used for marking the agent, but there could be an agent only if some being or object (explicit or understood) was being acted upon: in the equivalent of 'the man talks', the man was not treated as an agent. The working of all this is clarified if we think in terms of nominal predicates and parallel *talking of man* and *washing of linen*. Nouns designating objects or beings that were never conceived of as agents would not get a chance to receive the -*s* tag. We are so used to identifying agent and subject, that it is difficult for us to remember that an instrument as such can never be an agent. But the speakers of Proto-Indo-European would not have been misled into using the designation of the sieve (Lat. *cribrum*, OE. *hrīder* n.) in the ergative -*s* case; a sieve in action would, of course, be used in an instrumental case. IE. neuters are properly the nouns which, on account of their meanings, were never used in the ergative. As some linguists would put it, the absence of an -*s* form must have been *un fait de parole* before it became *un fait de langue*. A neuter noun like Latin *mare* is used as a bare stem both in *mare videt* 'he sees the sea' and *mare patet* 'the sea is to be seen', and this mirrors a former stage of Indo-European syntax.

The shift from a former ergative construction to the linguistic form with a compulsory subject, which we find in attested IE. languages, may have been determined by the development of the conjugation, a subject we cannot investigate here. The use of the -*s* form instead of the bare stem may have expanded first to constructions with intransitive verbs and ultimately to the properly nominative uses. The gradual elimination of the bare stem from its vocative uses and its replacement by the -*s* form is an historical process which is not quite completed yet: in Czech, for instance, the vocative *člověče* 'man!' is still distinct from the nominative *člověk* (whose -*s*, by an irony of fate, has long since disappeared). Formally this expansion of the -*s* form resulted in a twofold anomaly: the -*s* form was by now a subject, i.e. a form with no grammatical information any more, but with a functional mark still, and the bare stem of animate nouns, restricted now, in grammatical contexts, to the function of complement of transitive verbs, was deprived of any grammatical sign although its occurrence was somewhat less automatic than that of the formally marked subject. This latter aspect of the anomaly was soon remedied through the replacement of the bare-stem by a *to*-case in -*m*, the attested accusative (cf. Spanish 'direct' animate objects in *a*: *veo a Pablo* 'I see Paul'). This was analogically extended later to neuter *o*-stems.

The other lack of balance between information and cost was more difficult to eliminate: -*s* forms, the bulk of the new nominatives, were extremely frequent, early learned, and consequently resistant: if word final *s* dropped out at all, it could only be as the result of a regular phonological change, but not just in the particular cases where it was the nominative function marker. Its regular prehistoric elimination after sonants was welcome: it may well have been dropped only in certain contexts (utterance finally, for instance, or before consonant of a following word), but, if so, the forms without -*s* must have been eagerly extended by analogy to all positions. In thematic nouns, i.e. after the *e/o* vowel, it is well attested in many Indo-European branches. But, in later stages, whenever speakers are given a chance to choose, among phonologically regular forms between an -*s* form and an -*s*-less form, they give preference to the latter. Still, in many cases, centuries elapsed before phonological evolution offered any such chance: in French, one had to await the elimination of declension before -*s* singular nominatives yielded to -*s*-less oblique case forms.

In the lexical domain, abbreviation of segments whose frequency is on the increase does not raise problems, as a rule, if those segments are phrases of the *underground railway* type where the more general term can be left out and the specifier preserved as the equivalent of the whole. The reverse may also happen, the more general term being preserved, if the object that the phrase designates becomes so universal that the general term may be used, without any danger of confusion, as its normal designation: in most countries, motor-cars were first referred to as 'automobile carriages'; this phrase was soon curtailed to *automobile* and, finally to *auto*. But nowadays, after the practical elimination of all horse-drawn carriages, the usual designation of motor-cars is the old word for 'carriage'; Fr. *voiture*, Germ. *Wagen*, and so forth. If the designation is a learned word made up of elements that were significant in Latin or Greek, but make little sense for the average user of modern languages, the curtailing will be made at random, as far as etymology is concerned, but in such a way as to get a handy form whose size is well suited to its frequency and which rules out any danger of homonymic confusion.

Another frequent trick is the use of initials, as in LCC or USSR. These are particularly favoured among specialists, but are often resented, not only by purists, but by large sectors of the general public. Still they often represent the normal way out of some informational quandary: when the London County Council became a generally identified concept that had to be frequently referred to by many people, its frequency in speech became such that the cost of its full designation exceeded by far what corresponded to its, by then, fairly low informational value. No curtailing was possible since the combination of any two of its elements would have been misleading. The use of the three initials, probably first in writing, was certainly the most obvious and, in this complex world of ours, the most natural solution.

In common speech, where no spelling can suggest the use of initials, there may occur similar situations where none of the components can be left out, whatever the increase in frequency. Since the phonematic bulk cannot be reduced, speakers resort to a reduction of the morphological complexity and coagulate some of the elements into a single moneme or, at least, handle these elements grammatically as if they were one. The French phrase *avoir l'air* 'to look (like)' affords a nice illustration of coagulation in two successive stages. This phrase, in daily speech, must be about as frequent as its English equivalent and it has practically eliminated its traditional and literary competitors *sembler* and *paraître*. In its most usual form, the third person singular of the present *il a l'air* /ilaler/, it cannot be said to be phonologically more complex than what its frequency would lead us to expect, but its semantic articulation is cumbersome, as is shown by the behaviour of speakers: in 'unguarded' colloquial French, it is made to behave as a sort of copula; for 'she looks nice', one would expect *elle a l'air gentil*, with *gentil* agreeing with the masculine *air*; what one actually hears is *elle a l'air gentille*, with *gentille* agreeing in gender with the subject *elle*. With many children, the process of coagulation goes further: *air* is no longer identified as a noun, but as the second syllable of the stem *alair-* /aler-/ of a regular -*er* verb **alairer*, hence, in the imperfect, *ça m'alairait bon*, 'it looked good to me', instead of standard *ça m'avait l'air bon*.

We have, so far, been considering what happens to a form when its frequency increases. In cases where it decreases, we have pointed out that this does not necessarily involve any formal change provided no homonymic conflict arises. But a lowering of the frequency which, in itself, would not endanger the survival of a form, may seal its doom if it is somehow isolated in the structure, if, for instance, it is a verb that is not inflected according to a widespread analogical pattern. When children learn their language, they tend to imitate comparatively long stretches they have heard before they are able to analyse them, i.e. to use in other contexts the elements they contain. As long as they do not use analogy, which amounts to contriving new moneme combinations, they have no problems with irregular forms. But when they start doing it extensively, which, with the average child, will begin about the age of five, they will be apt to replace an irregular and isolated *brought* by an analogical *brung*. Irregular forms that are very frequent are, by that time, well entrenched, and occasional slips like *brung* will eventually disappear. But those whose frequency is somewhat lower will be widely mishandled. If the community is not of a conservative type, children will be allowed to use their own forms, and analogical forms will finally get established. If, on the contrary, adults insist on correcting children, the latter will try to avoid the forms they do not know how to inflect to the satisfaction of their elders; these trouble-makers will become obsolescent and eventually disappear. English *move* was borrowed from French and was from the start inflected according to most general analogical patterns. It is today one of the most frequently used lexical items of the English language. The original French *mouvoir* must have had, from early times, a number of unusual inflexional features. In any case, there is today no other verb conjugated just like it. It is about as peculiar in its inflexional comportment as *pouvoir* or *vouloir*, yet it must always have been somewhat less frequent than these quasi-auxiliaries, and the amount of irregularity which speakers could cope with in handling these proved a little too high for *mouvoir*. As a result, *mouvoir* has disappeared from colloquial French; the normal equivalents of 'move' are *remuer*, *bouger*, *déménager*, all single-stem *-er* verbs; another literary equivalent of *move* is *émouvoir* which survives, in speech, only as an infinitive and two participles: *émouvant* and *ému*; but even these are threatened by the forms of the denominative single-stem *émotionner*.[1]

We have so far, in the case of significant units, been operating with general frequency. But in order to understand how language works and changes, it is quite essential to operate with frequency or, better, probability in given contexts: *book* and *walk* are frequent words, but a combination like *the book walks* is quite unexpected and either nonsensical or highly informative because it is quite improbable. In other words, the informative value of *the book walks* is higher than what a calculation based upon the general frequency of *book* and that of *walk* might lead us to expect. On the other hand, *blue* and *sky* are so frequently used together that *blue sky* contributes less information than the average probability of *blue* and that of *sky* would suggest. According to whether the speaker or the writer wants to startle his public or, on the contrary, to flatter his laziness and conservatism, he will try to find unexpected combinations, or use time-hallowed phrases and turns. Generally speaking, cultured audiences or publics are those who, at the same time, are able to digest more information per second, and need more unexpected combinations in order to get the same amount of information, since they hear new turns more often and consequently find them much sooner hackneyed and stale. It is thus clear that style is largely a matter of density of information, and this covers to a large extent the subject-matter of the experience, real or fictive, which is communicated, since the understanding and appreciation of literary communication implies previously shared experience, and shared experience implies familiarity with a certain vocabulary. Whether communication is of a literary nature or just an everyday spoken

---

[1] For an illustration of the working of formal analogy, see 'De l'économie des formes du verbe en français parlé', *Studia . . . in hon. L. Spitzer*, pp. 315 ff.

affair, it involves a constant renewal of the details of linguistic practice, because every one of us, author or speaker,
will find it necessary to emphasize some segments of his
utterances through additional information resulting from
unexpected collocations. If the trick proves successful, the
inventor himself or some of his hearers will be tempted to
use it again, and the new turn may get established in the
language. But should it become too popular, it would soon
lose all its efficiency and be replaced by some fresh innova-
tion. There are, at all times, large sections of the vocabulary
that are in a constant state of unrest, and since all the parts
of a language condition one another, we find here a permanent cause of linguistic evolution.

It is tempting to try to reduce all linguistic facts to quantitative data, as we have been doing. But we should not forget
that what we may call the nature or quality of the various
linguistic units plays an essential role in the conditioning of
linguistic evolution: what can be measured is the quantity,
not the quality of information. If a new word enters a
language, its appearance will necessarily modify the informational economy of that language. If there were n words
before, there will now be $n+1$ words. In theory, every one
of the n words should have become less frequent in the process. But, in fact, the frequency of all but very few of the
n words will not be affected. Only those whose meaning is in
some way connected to that of the new-comer are likely to
score a lower probability. The impact of the lexical expansion will be limited to a certain semantic domain. Besides, we
cannot be satisfied with the statement that the appearance of
a new word A has reduced by so much the probability of a
formerly existing word B, because this does not tell us what
semantic field remains allotted to it and what section of its
former domain has been encroached upon by A. This we
need to know if we want to understand the further repercussions of the adoption of A. In the field of phonology, we have

seen that a similar frequency of geminates and corresponding single consonants is only one of the factors that determined the simplification of the geminates: this simplification can only occur if no dangerous confusion will ensue, which largely depends on the phonic nature of the other units of the system. All this means that applying the statistical technique of informational research to language should not make us forget that semantic and phonic properties of linguistic units cannot be disregarded when problems of evolution are at issue. The importance of the implications for our research of recently evolved methods of investigation should not entail a disregard of previous efforts towards the understanding of semantic evolution.[1]

As regards phonology, whole-hearted attempts at establishing a structural method of diachronic investigation are comparatively recent, and they have, if not from the start, at least very early, involved informational considerations.[2] A basic problem, with phonological changes, is to explain how the changing needs of man can affect the second articulation of language, one of the main functions of which is precisely to make the phonic form independent of the semantic value of the message and of its significant components. The hypothesis that frequency could modify cost, i.e. exert an influence on the form of the units, phonemes as well as monemes, suggested that this was at least one of the channels through which communicative needs could act upon the economy of phonematic patterns. Yet there are other channels, and we must keep in mind the role played by prosodical features such as accent and intonation which, being direct responses to communicative needs, are most likely links between these and the phonemes.[3] But what is probably more important than determining how external factors of unbalance pene-

---

[1] Cf. Suzanne Öhman's survey paper 'Theories of the "Linguistic Field" ', *Word*, ix (1953), pp. 123–34.

[2] See *Économie*, pp. 139–47.

[3] Cf. *Manual of Phonetics*, ed. by Louise Kaiser (Amsterdam, 1957), pp. 255–62.

trate the system is the examination of the repercussions of
that unbalance within the system. When trying to account
for past linguistic changes, on any one of the planes of
language, there will come a point where we will be at a loss
to go farther for lack of precise historical information. It is not
suggested here that we should not try to cull useful hints
wherever we can find them, but we shall achieve the best
results if we concentrate on a domain we know well and are
best equipped to investigate, namely language structure in
all its aspects.

INDEX OF SUBJECTS

M

tones, 30–31, 33–34.
triangular vowel patterns, 79.

universals (relational), 58.

variation (as a characteristic of language), 23.
variation of *signifiant*, 91–93.
variations within one community, 106–7.

verb, 49, 65, 100–1.
vocal chords, 27, 28, 29.
vocal nature of speech, 25.
voice, 31.
voice (of verbs), 49, 51, 101.

word, 90, 92.
word order (relevancy of), 41, 64.
writing, 25–26.
written *v.* spoken language, 122.

INDEX OF LANGUAGES

INDEX OF AUTHORS

PRINTED IN GREAT BRITAIN
AT THE UNIVERSITY PRESS, OXFORD
BY VIVIAN RIDLER
PRINTER TO THE UNIVERSITY